REFUTING THE NEW ATHEISTS

REFUTING THE NEW ATHEISTS

A CHRISTIAN RESPONSE
TO SAM HARRIS,
CHRISTOPHER HITCHENS, &
RICHARD DAWKINS

DOUGLAS WILSON

canonpress
Moscow, Idaho

Douglas Wilson, *Refuting the New Atheists: A Christian Response to Sam Harris, Christopher Hitchens, and Richard Dawkins*
Copyright ©2021 by Douglas Wilson.
Published by Canon Press
P.O. Box 8729, Moscow, Idaho 83843

This edition includes *Letter from a Christian Citizen: A Response to Sam Harris's Letter to a Christian Nation*; *God Is: How Christianity Explains Everything*; and *The Deluded Atheist: A Response to Richard Dawkins's The God Delusion*. First edition of *Letter from a Christian Citizen* published 2007 by American Vision, Powder Springs, Georgia. Second edition published 2019 by Blog & Mablog Press. First edition of *God Is* published 2008 by American Vision, Powder Springs, Georgia. Second edition published 2019 by Blog & Mablog Press. First edition of *The Deluded Atheist* published 2008 by American Vision, Powder Springs, Georgia. Second edition published 2019 by Blog and Mablog Press.

Cover design by James Engerbretson. Interior layout by Valerie Anne Bost. Printed in the United States of America.

Library of Congress Cataloging-in-Publication Data forthcoming

21 22 23 21 22 23 24 25 26   10 9 8 7 6 5 4 3 2

CONTENTS

LETTER FROM A CHRISTIAN CITIZEN

A RESPONSE TO SAM HARRIS'S *LETTER TO A CHRISTIAN NATION*

CHAPTER 1

DEAR MR. HARRIS

I would love to begin by saying something like
"Greetings in the Lord," but I have no idea what
your background is or whether you have ever been
baptized. And so, not to presume, let me begin simply
by greeting you warmly in a general fashion and thank-
ing you for setting your thoughts down so plainly. I
would also hope that I might raise some equally clear
questions about what you have written.

On the first page of your small book, you begin by
discussing some of the reaction you got to your first
book, *The End of Faith*. You say that the "most hostile"
responses came to you from Christians. "The truth is
that many who claim to be transformed by Christ's love

are deeply, even murderously, intolerant of criticism"
(vii).[1] You suggest the possibility that this might just
be attributable to human nature, but you don't think
so. You go on to suggest that "such hatred" draws
"considerable support from the Bible." You say your
reason for saying this is that the "most disturbed of
my correspondents always cite chapter and verse" (vii).

I think I know why you began your book this way. I
have been in evangelical Christian circles my entire life,
and one of the *standard* concerns that many Christians
have is presenting "a bad testimony" to nonbelievers.
Of course this doesn't prevent some Christians from
presenting that bad testimony anyway, oblivious to all
surrounding concerns. But your opening is guaranteed
to cause many Christian readers to lament the fact that
a number of professing Christians have sought to clob-
ber you for Christ through their hostility. And then
when you didn't respond favorably to "the treatment,"
these sorts of people have another chapter and verse
handy that can explain *that*.

You opened your book this way because you knew
(quite accurately) that Christians generally would be
upset by it, would be put on the defensive, would be
sorrowful over what some of us have done to you in
the name of Christ, and so on. I know, and you clearly know, that Christians can behave badly in this way,

---

1. Throughout this book, the page numbers given in parentheses refer to Sam Harris, *Letter to a Christian Nation* (New York: Random House, 2006).

and you also knew that a lot of other Christians would be ashamed of this undeniable fact. And you are right: we are ashamed of this kind of thing. When my son (a Christian) published an article showing how the Shroud of Turin could easily have been produced with medieval off-the-shelf technology,[2] he got lots of mail—from professing Christians—with all sorts of variants of "go to hell" or "I hope you rot in hell." So you tagged us. The Christian Church has a problem with this kind of person in our midst. We are embarrassed by it, believing it to be inconsistent with what Christ taught and what we profess to believe. Attributing it to human nature doesn't cut it with us because we believe that Christ came to transform human nature. You knew this about us and started out very shrewdly. You knew that we would disapprove of this kind of thing, just as you do.

But *that*, actually, was the surprising thing: that you, too, disapproved of that kind of hateful behavior. You used a number of words that clearly portrayed that disapproval: hostile, murderously, disturbed, hatred. I could not get to your second page without encountering a cluster of indignant moral judgments, and I am genuinely curious as to what you could possibly offer as the basis for these judgments. Pick the nastiest letter you got from the nastiest Christian out there. As a pastor, I know what I would say to him about it because I

---

2. Books and Culture, March/April 2005, Volume 11, Number 2, pp. 22–29. The article can now be found online.

can appeal to the Bible. But what could *you* say to him? By your understanding of the world, he is just doing his thing. Two hundred years from now, when both you and he have returned to the soil, what difference will it make? There is no judgment, no standard, no law that overarches the two of you. When this nasty Christian dies, you don't even have the satisfaction of knowing that he will finally discover the error of his ways. He will discover nothing of the kind. You believe his eyes will close and that will be that. The material universe will not give everyone thirty minutes after death to re-adjust their thoughts on the subject before they pass into final oblivion. So why, on your terms, should he have written you a nice letter? *I* think he should have, but then again, I'm the pastor guy.

In different ways, this same issue is going to come up again and again as I respond to various portions of your book. You want Christians to quit behaving in certain ways. But why? You want them to write nice letters to atheist authors, and you want them to stop turning America into a big, dumb theocracy. But *why*? If there is no God, what could *possibly* be wrong with theocracies? They provide high entertainment value, and they give everybody involved in them a sense of dignity and high moral purpose. They get to wear ecclesiastical robes, march in impressive processions to burn intransigent people at the stake, believing they are better than everybody else and that God likes them. Further, the material universe doesn't care about any of this foolishness, not even a little bit. So what's wrong with having a little bit of fun at the expense of other bits of protoplasm? Hitler, Ronald Reagan, Pol Pot, Mother Teresa, Mao, Nancy Pelosi, Stalin, Ted Haggard, and the Grand Inquisitor are all just part of a gaudy and very temporary show. Sometimes the Northern lights put on a show in the sky. Sometimes people put on a show on the ground. Then the sun goes out and, behold, nobody cares. Given your premises, this is the way it has to be.

But I find it quite curious that you clearly do care what happens to our nation. "The primary purpose of the book is to arm secularists in our society, who believe that religion should be kept out of public policy, against their opponents on the Christian Right" (viii). Again, you are using words like *should be*. Not only do you have an *ought* going here, you have one that you are clearly willing to impose on others who differ with you (which can be seen in your goal of "arming" secularists). But what is the difference between an imposed morality, an imposed religion, or an imposed secular *ought*? Why is your imposition to be preferred to any other?

Although your book is small, the goal is certainly ambitious. "In *Letter to a Christian Nation*, I have set out to demolish the intellectual and moral pretensions of Christianity in its most committed forms" (ix). In order to demolish something intellectually, you have to have a standard for thought and reason, and I presume you will reveal this standard later in your book so we will be able to discuss it. But you also want to demolish the moral pretensions of the Christian faith. This could have two meanings. You might mean to show that Christianity does not live up to its own professed standard, in which case you are simply joining a long covenant tradition of admonishing hypocrisy that includes the prophet Amos and John the Baptist. I could not really object to this, because it is what I try to do every Sunday in the pulpit. But you appear to mean something else. You seem to be saying that there is a standard which Christianity does not acknowledge even though it is authoritative over Christians anyway, and that Christianity is in rebellion against this standard. I want to continue to ask you for the source of this standard. Who has defined this standard? You? Your friends? Is it published somewhere so I can read it? You write as though it exists. Where is it?

You say, "In *Letter to a Christian Nation*, however, I engage Christianity at its most divisive, injurious, and retrograde" (ix). So Christianity is divisive, compared to what standard for unity? Who promulgated this standard? Why do we have to submit to it? Christianity is injurious, you say, but I would want to inquire why it is bad to be injurious. What standard do you appeal to here? And *retrograde* means that we are sliding backwards in some sense. What slope are we sliding down? Why are we not allowed to slide down it? I am not trying to be cute here. I think these are the central questions in this discussion. Okay, so I am part of a *divisive, injurious* and *retrograde* movement. Is that bad?

At the conclusion of your "Note to the Reader," you make an opening move in what I suppose is part of your larger strategy of demolishing the "intellectual pretensions of Christianity." You begin by noting that the intellectual pretensions of the Christian faith are certainly widespread. "If our worldview were put to a vote, notions of 'intelligent design' would defeat the science of biology by nearly three to one" (x). I do not share the same faith you apparently do in the abilities of pollsters to measure this sort of thing, but let us grant this as at least a distinct possibility. You believe that the pervasiveness of certain Christian doctrines constitutes "a moral and intellectual emergency" (xii). You speak in terms of "us and them," so allow me to do the same thing for a moment. You all have had nearly complete control of the education establishment for over a century and a half. You have the accrediting agencies, you have the government schools, and you have the vast majority of colleges and universities. You *are* the educational establishment. And yet your complaint here reminds me of the indignant father who said, "I taught him everything I know and he's *still* stupid!" At what point should a committed secularist take responsibility for the state of education in America? Perhaps the problem is not in the students?

But there is more to this argument. It is quite true that I do not regard the widespread acceptance of intelligent design as indicating stupidity, apathy, or worse. I believe God created the world, and His intelligence is on display in riotous ways in everything I look at every day. But given the current climate, this conviction is certainly easy to *mock*:

> This means that despite a full century of scientific insights attesting to the antiquity of the earth, more than half of our neighbors believe that the entire cosmos was created six thousand years ago. This is, incidentally, about a thousand years after the Sumerians invented glue. (x–xi)

But notice what you are doing here: the Sumerians *invented* glue? Glue didn't just happen? Why couldn't it just appear the way the sexuality of moss, and the eyeballs that see in color, and the superbly engineered ankle, and the majesty of the great white sharks all did? *Glue* is so complicated that it needed to be invented?

You say that our nation is a "dim-witted giant" (xi). You say that we combine "great power and great stupidity" (xi). To bring this installment to a close, let me just give you a friendly caution. This sort of thing is probably red meat to many of the folks buying your books. But if you are really concerned about delivering our nation from our Christian "clutches," I am afraid that underestimating the intelligence and education of your foes will probably not help you at all in the long run.

CHAPTER 2

A TROUT IN THE PUNCHBOWL

I n your first argument (3–7), you begin the discussion with agreement. That agreement may seem minimal to some, but I actually believe that a great deal rides on it. The agreement is that one of us must be right and the other wrong. There either is a God or there is not. As you put it, "We agree, for instance, that if one of us is right, the other is wrong. The Bible is either the word of God or it isn't. Either Jesus offers humanity the one, true path to salvation (John 14:6), or he does not" (3). This is an appropriate way to state it and a good place to begin. Some might claim this is a false dichotomy, but it really is a fair statement.

If I say the car must either be red or green, I am leaving a lot of other possibilities out. But if I say the car must either be red or not red, I have pretty much covered the waterfront.

So we agree. Jesus is either the divine Son of God or He is not. Jesus either died on the cross as a sacrifice for the sins of humanity or He did not. I will return to the implications of this in a future section.

But, not surprisingly, we then part company. You say, "Consider: every devout Muslim has *the same reasons* for being a Muslim that you have for being a Christian" (6, emphasis mine). You advance an argument that might be called an argument for partial atheism: "The truth is, you know exactly what it is like to be an atheist with respect to the beliefs of Muslims" (7). But I am afraid that this is a false analogy entirely. You say, "Understand that the way you view Islam is precisely the way devout Muslims view Christianity. And it is the way I view all religions" (7). Well, no, not exactly. And well, actually, no, not at all.

Suppose we are considering a phenomenon that is, by *most* accounts, inexplicable as an unsupervised occurrence—three of us attend a sophisticated party uptown, and halfway through the evening at the party, we find a trout in the punchbowl. At this point, the three of us divide into three schools of thought. I think that Smith, a practical joker, put it there; our friend Murphy thinks that Jones, the *avant garde* performance artist, put it there; and you think that it has simply shown up as the result of natural forces. My central point is not to interact with the truth or falsity of your naturalistic position—except perhaps through the use of this absurd example of the punchbowl—but rather to show that you are arguing for something *completely different* from what Murphy and I are arguing. Each of us has an explanation, but your explanation is of a different kind altogether.

The difference between two of us (between Murphy and me) concerns *who* put the trout in the punchbowl. The difference between the both of us together and you is over *whether* someone put a trout in the punchbowl. And *who* and *whether* represent different questions entirely. Quite apart from who is right and who is wrong about this, it is important to note that we are not disagreeing in the same way or over the same kind of issue at all. Murphy and I are disagreeing about the relative behaviors of Smith and Jones, but not over whether the trout calls for an explanation. Maybe I am more hostile to Smith than I ought to be, and maybe Murphy is deeply prejudiced against Jones. Maybe we are both wrong about who put it there. But thinking that someone's explanation is inadequate (when we agree the phenomenon *must* be explained) is quite different from arguing with someone who says that it calls for no outside explanation whatever.

When a general wants to fight a battle, he also wants to pick the terrain. Being able to choose the location is always a significant advantage. Likewise, the way a debate is structured will often affect the outcome of that debate. So we need to begin our discussion by noting that your structure for this debate needs to be completely revised. Rejecting a proffered explanation is totally different from saying there is no need for an explanation. In short, your unbelief in the Christian faith is *not* the same kind of thing at all as my unbelief in Islam. And I am not a "partial atheist" because I am not a Muslim. You say, "No one needed to put the world here." The Muslim says that Allah created it. I say that the triune God did. These statements contradict one another in different ways—not *in the same way*, as you argued.

I admitted above that the trout in the punchbowl was an absurd example, but before wrapping this up, I want to make sure my admission is not taken the wrong way. I was not confessing that I was attempting a straw man argument. By such examples I am not trying to make your position *look* absurd; rather, I am trying to communicate something of the wonder Christians feel when we look at virtually anything in the real world. A trout in the punchbowl would certainly surprise me, but really no more than do hummingbird wings, the conveyor belt in our ears that slowly carries the wax out, pine cones that don't do any reproductive good until a forest fire pops them open, the carefully perforated edge around a housefly pupa that doesn't come open until a blood bag comes out of the fly's head to push it open, or an acorn that has the ability to make a huge oak tree out of what it finds in the air. The trout in the punch actually requires far less explaining than any of these things. So the absurdity of my example is actually that it falls so far short.

You might respond by saying that since the punchbowl was filled at 6:30 and we arrived at the party around 7:15, this did not give the laws of nature any *time* to do their usual magic. The evolution of life on our planet, you might say, required many millions of years to accomplish what it has. But if we are talking about matter organizing itself up a cliff face with no pitons or boots at a strenuous climb, additional time only makes the problems worse. Miracles don't go any better if you roll the tape in slow motion. Ice cubes bumping together won't make a trout, and I can't evade the difficulties inherent in the theory by postulating an additional hundred years for the ice cubes to bump in. If I wanted to walk across the swimming pool, I do not increase my chances by inching out onto the water *slowly*. This means that your account of the trout in the punchbowl is tenuous whether you have a lot of time or not very much time.

But in *either* case, whether we are dealing with eons or minutes, your naturalistic explanation of how a trout might have gotten there remains a very different kind of explanation than those given by people who believe *someone* had to put it there.

CHAPTER 3

PLAYING TO THE CHEAP SEATS

Your next argument does not appear to be an argument proper at all, but rather a marshaling of "scary quotes" from the Old Testament. These are set against certain contemporary assumptions about law and justice, and you do this on the safe bet that most of your readers will not go back and question any of those assumptions. But I think it would be really helpful if someone were actually to do that. Some of your assumptions do not appear to have been asked a question in years.

You cite various biblical laws that have offended your sensibilities (Prov. 13:24, 20:30, and 23:13–14; Exod. 21:15; Lev. 20:9; Deut. 21:18–21; Mark 7:9–13;

Matt. 15:4–7; Deut. 13:6, 8–15). You point out (quite *correctly*, I might add) that Jesus was not in the least bit embarrassed by any of this. You cite Matthew 5:18–19 to establish this point, but it would have strengthened your argument significantly to use Mark 7:10 where Jesus expressly refers to one of the scary parts of the Old Testament (the penalty for cursing parents), and He does so with an unapologetic affirmation.

You cite 2 Thessalonians 1:6–9 and John 15:6 to show (again rightly) that the New Testament does not represent what could be called a softening of the ethics of the Old Testament. Grace and love and supreme kindness characterize the New Testament, that is true, but these are also found in the Old Testament. Law and judgment are indeed found in the Old Testament, but these are found in *heightened* form in the New Testament. So you are correct. It is false to say that the Old Testament represents severity and the New Testament represents kindness. Both are found in the Old Testament, and both are found in accentuated form in the New Testament. The judgments that fall in the Old Testament are largely temporal judgments. The judgments that Jesus speaks of are eternal. Out of all the teachers and prophets in the Bible, the preeminent hellfire and damnation preacher is the Lord Jesus Himself. You rightly see that the Old and New Testaments stand or fall together.

But then, instead of demonstrating why they must *fall* together, you simply make an appeal to the nickel seats. You bring up laws and customs involving cultures thousands of years away from us, and you use the "outlandish" aspects of these customs to frighten modernists who don't get out much. For example, without providing any context you cite a passage that you say allows a father to sell his daughter "into sexual slavery" (Exod. 21:7–11). But what this law actually represents is an amelioration of an existing custom, and the law placed bounds and restrictions on that custom to keep abuses from becoming outrages. The same kind of thing happened with polygamy—not approved as such, but restricted and bounded. But while we are on the subject of sexual slavery, let me raise the question of whether anything like that is occurring now. Are there fathers who pimp their daughters today? Well, yes, but when it happens, we are probably talking about an MTV reality show and the general approval from the fans of cultural degradation. But if that is not explicit enough, then let's talk about sexual slavery of *children* in places like Thailand. And let's ask who would be most likely to approve of sexual jaunts to visit the slaves there—your average believer in the Old Testament laws you dismissively cite or people who share your opinions about rejecting the Old Testament law? Are there special airfare rates from San Francisco, do you think?

You didn't limit your discussion to sexual slavery though. You gave us several passages where the apostle Paul "admonishes slaves to serve their masters well—and to serve their Christian masters especially well" (16). You cite Ephesians 6:5 and 1 Timothy 6:1–4, which make your point plainly enough. Unlike some of the Old Testament passages you cited, your representation of these passages was fairly accurate. St. Paul *did* teach Christian slaves to work hard. He taught Christian masters to remember that they had a master in Heaven, and this presupposes that there were Christian masters who were members of his churches. He did teach Christian slaves to make a special point of working diligently for believing masters. Now here is my question: Given your worldview, what is wrong with this? There is nothing wrong with it on your principles, where the universe is just time and chance acting on matter. Why does it matter if the master matter acts on the slave matter? Who cares?

From our Christian perspective, the apostle was subverting the *entire* pagan system—and taking it down with the pagan system of slavery included in the demolition job. He did not do this by revolutionary means, but rather by means of the Christian gospel. Biblical subversion of pagan slavery was not violent, but rather worked the same way that yeast works through a loaf of bread. Promoting the ethic of a new world, a new Heaven and a new earth, was what the apostle Paul was after, and slavery was radically inconsistent with this vision. A very good description of the Pauline strategy in this can be found in N.T. Wright's commentary on Philemon, the letter in which Paul is returning a runaway slave.[3]

But from an atheistic perspective, how can slavery be consistently condemned? You don't really address this question at all, but rather engage in some ethical hand waving. "Nothing in Christian theology remedies the appalling deficiencies of the Bible on what is perhaps the greatest—and the *easiest*—moral question our society has ever had to face" (18). All right. You say this is the easiest moral question that our society has ever faced. Okay then, that sounded confident. This must be a *really* easy question for you to answer. You asserted this, but then you did not answer it. Given your principles, why is slavery wrong? The Christian view is that all mankind is created in the image of God, and that Christ came to liberate us from our slavery to sin and restore that image. It is easy to see on these principles how slavery is not what God intends for us. Christ came to proclaim liberty for the captives (Luke 4:18). The Bible prohibits the manstealing that was the foundation of the slave trade (1 Tim. 1:10). In Christ there is neither Jew nor Greek, male nor female, slave nor free (Gal. 3:28). The logic of the new creation in Christ provides liberation from the slavery of sin, which is the foundation of all other forms of slavery (Gal. 5:1). But how could *atheism* lead to a condemnation of slavery?

---

3. N.T. Wright, *Colossians and Philemon* (Grand Rapids, MI: Eerdmans, 1986), 164–192.

You make a superficial attempt to answer the question, but it really answers nothing, and addresses nothing.

> The moment a person recognizes that slaves are human beings like himself, enjoying the same capacity for suffering and happiness, he will understand that it is patently evil to own them and treat them like farm equipment. (18–19)

This appears to be an argument that nerve endings disqualify one from being a slave or being treated like farm equipment. But what about farm *animals?* They have nerve endings, and they certainly have a capacity for suffering. This anticipates the problem you have with your approval of Jain ethics, but I will address this shortly.

Secondly, you simply throw random texts at your readers, and expect them to react with indignation. This is easy to do because in Old Testament societies, when criminal or financial offenses were committed, the options that they had were execution, exile, fines, flogging, and slavery. These options are there, right in the text. But out of this list of five, we still practice three of them in our nation today—execution, fines, and slavery. If a noncitizen is involved, we still practice a fourth—exile (calling it deportation). The only sentence that is not used in our nation today is flogging.

You might object to my assertion that we still have slavery. But notice what our Constitution says about it. "Neither slavery nor involuntary servitude, *except as a punishment* for crime whereof the party shall have been duly convicted, shall exist within the United States, or any place subject to their jurisdiction" (U.S. Constitution, Article XIII.i, emphasis mine). And this is not a punishment that we resort to on rare occasions either. There over *two million* people currently incarcerated in the United States. You think that slavery is gone because on your way to work you don't drive by anybody involuntarily toiling in the cotton fields. That is because *our* system of slavery has been to build a massive network of kennels to store people out of sight in six by eight cells. You might say that, yes, these people are restricted in their liberty, but they were convicted of crimes. Yes, many of them were, and every society has a right to protect itself, ours included, and so perhaps you ought not to ride a high horse when it comes to ancient societies protecting themselves as well.

But even with allowances made in this way, I want to press the point—we are not dealing with two million murderers, rapists, or violent offenders. Quite a few of the inhabitants of these secularist kennels of yours were idiot teenagers with bags of pot, and they were sent off to these graduate schools of crime and vice from courtrooms that were as secular as anything someone like you could desire. In these courtrooms, if an attorney were to quote the Ten Commandments or the Golden Rule with any kind of approval, the judge would wet his pants. You told us that this was an easy moral question. Why haven't we solved it yet? Why does the United States house two million slaves? That is *twice* the entire population of the state I live in. Given this, your easy dismissal of biblical ethics is just that—far too easy. "Anyone who believes the Bible offers the best guidance we have on questions of morality has some very strange ideas about either guidance or morality" (14).

This brings us back to your basis for morality, which was basically pleasure and pain. "Questions of morality are questions about happiness and suffering. This is why you and I do not have moral obligations toward rocks" (8). Okay. *Whose* happiness and suffering? Why ought one individual, with one set of nerve endings, be concerned about another set of nerve endings entirely? They are not connected except through cultural teaching. That teaching, in our case, is grounded in the will of God. In your case, it is grounded in bare assertion. What you need to do here is sketch for us the bridge between one set of nerve endings and another, and show us why that bridge of yours creates an obligation those two sets of nerve endings must share. You say this is obvious, so it should not take that long to explain. "There are obvious biological reasons why people tend to treat their parents well, and to think badly of murderers, adulterers, thieves, and liars" (21). Obvious biological reasons? A Mother's Day card proceeds from the same kind of impulse that causes me to scratch an itch or go to the bathroom? *Biological* reasons? There are also obvious biological reasons that might run the other way, that go into adultery, for example. You really need to explain this further.

One last thing. You refer to the "obscene celebrations of violence that we find throughout the Old and New Testaments" (11). You set this over against the "utter non-violence" of Jainism, a religion originating in ancient India which you praise highly. This is frankly mystifying. You say the morality of the Jains surpasses the morality of the Christians, and you cite a Jain tenet. "Do not injure, abuse, oppress, enslave, insult, torment, torture, or kill any creature or living being" (23). I really cannot figure this out. You are an atheist, an *evolutionist*. And yet you praise the morality of utter non-violence, which would have gotten the evolutionary struggle absolutely nowhere. Devout Jains will go barefoot all the time to avoid stepping on bugs and will carry a broom to sweep the path in front of them all the time, for the same reason. Devout Jains will wear a mask to avoid breathing in and thereby killing any insect. You say this represents a superior morality to that of the Christians who believe in the Bible. So you are saying—as an atheist—that if America's evangelical Christians all forsook the use of antibiotics because of the genocidal devastation it was causing to the microbes within, you would *commend* us for the moral advance? Do you promise? Because it seems to me that it would be a golden opportunity for you to dismiss us all as uneducated nutjobs.

This is a response to just a few pages from your book, and it represents one of the central problems that I see in how you are arguing your case. You are raising far more questions than you are answering, and yet you are raising them as though they were already answered. And I think this, again, is just playing to the cheap seats.

CHAPTER 4

SO WHAT'S WRONG WITH TIN FOIL ICE CREAM?

I was very interested in your section called "Real Morality" (23–32) because I believe that atheism is at its weakest when it comes to finding a decent foundation for *oughts* and *shoulds*. In this section you sought to establish an objective basis for morality apart from the authority of a divine being. In addition to this, you sought to critique various aspects of Christian morality. Not surprisingly, I believe your argument failed on both counts.

Your critique of Christian morality is what I would like to deal with first, because your critique involved some astounding internal contradictions. For example, you attack the evangelical opposition to embryonic stem cell research. "A three-day-old human embryo is a collection of 150 cells called a blastocyst" (29). You compared this to the number of cells in a common household fly and ridiculed evangelical deficiencies when it came to moral proportionality. Now I differ with this criticism, but it is at least a cogent argument. But what I could not reconcile was this critique with your earlier praise of the Jains in the previous section. You commended them for their commitment to *absolute* nonviolence. As I mentioned, devout Jains will sweep the path in front of them to keep from killing the bugs. Their commitment to nonviolence includes a commitment to nonviolence against, say, malarial mosquitoes. You imply that if evangelicals would get behind the medical use of embryonic stem cells, then much greater good would come of it. (By the way, I am here concerned simply with the *structure* of your argument. Whether the "promise" of embryonic stem cell research can live up to the current whooping for funding is a question for another time.) But why are the Jains not condemned for this same reason? Why is their unwillingness to take out mosquitoes on a par with the evangelical respect for the life of the blastocyst? Why do you not praise the evangelicals for taking a small step, however small, toward a universal respect for all life? Just like the Jains?

Your inconsistency here is why you could say something like this: "This explains why Christians like yourself expend more 'moral' energy opposing abortion than fighting genocide" (25). Please know that to Christian ears a statement like this sounds like: "When are you Christians going to stop defending Jews and join us in opposing the *real* holocausts around the globe?" Such a statement would reveal perhaps more than the speaker intended, implying that killing Jews does not qualify as a real holocaust. On Christian terms, opposing abortion *is* fighting genocide. When you chide us for fighting abortion instead of genocide you reveal your assumption that unborn children are not human beings—for if they were, killing them by the millions would be genocide, would it not?

But even on Jain terms, praised highly by you just a few pages earlier, abortion can certainly be opposed because our respect should extend to "any creature or living being." Your moral calculus has been cast thus far in terms of advancing happiness and avoiding pain and suffering. You praised, in glowing terms, the length to which Jains would go to avoid doing injury to *any* living creature. We saw that this includes wearing face masks to avoid breathing in a bug. Now would you care to compare the suffering of a breathed-in bug to the suffering of a late term fetus, the victim of a partial-birth abortion? And would you care to explain why you call Christians fanatics for opposing such slaughter of unborn children, but point to Jains as moral exemplars for protecting bugs?

You mock Christian concerns over the human soul, reducing it to a question of *size*. "The naive idea of souls in a Petri dish is intellectually indefensible . . . . Your beliefs about the human soul are, at this very moment, prolonging the scarcely endurable misery of tens of millions of human beings" (31). There are two problems here. First, in blunt terms, you are prepared to sacrifice the small for the sake of the large, not having learned the important lesson taught by *Horton Hears a Who*, that a "person's a person, no matter how small." But at the same time this oversight is not consistent at all. You are prepared to praise those who defend the small, provided that the defender is not a Christian. This betrays your prejudice against Christians, regardless of what they do. It appears that your interest is to throw something at the Christians, and you don't really seem to mind what it is so long as it's hard.

The second problem is that you engaged in a little sleight of hand here. You don't believe in the human soul in the petri dish, that's true enough. But you also don't believe in the human soul when it is encased in one J.S. Bach and is busy composing the Brandenburg Concertos. You make as though it is incredible to believe that a small cluster of cells can be ensouled, but your real issue is that you believe that no one has a soul. Right? We are all bags of complex chemical reactions—whether 150 cells or ten trillion of them is just a matter of how big the sack is. But then you demand to know why we won't sacrifice the blastocysts for the sake "tens of millions of human beings." Human beings? What are those?

Your book so far has been filled with many moral judgments and assessments, and given your denial of God's existence, how you justify this is a matter of some interest. Your basis for objective morality (*sans* God) basically amounts to an appeal to the capacity for happiness and pain respectively. "For there to be objective moral truths worth knowing, there need only be better and worse ways to seek happiness in this world" (23). But in order for this moral calculus to work, it has to be aligned with what it is based on. If it is based on the nervous system and the capacity for pain and pleasure, then it extends just as far as that nervous system does and no farther. A moral standard contrary to what brings one nervous system pleasure is a standard that can be rejected by *that* nervous system out of hand. You try to say that love is better than hate, all things considered. But this is like saying that since most people like vanilla ice cream, manufacturers make far more vanilla than the kind that has chunks of tin foil in it. Okay. But making "the ice cream less eaten" would not be a *moral* issue. It is just a question of what most people like. Not only is this so, but we could also point out that in certain portions of the world, the tin foil ice cream appears to be enjoying robust sales.

This is how you describe it:

Everything about human experience suggests that love is more conducive to happiness than hate is. This is an objective claim about the human mind, about the dynamics of social relations, and about the moral order of our world. (24)

Three questions come to mind. First, why is this not a question of preferences instead of morality? What's the difference between individual preferences and moral choices? Second, if "everything about human experience" shows that love is better than hate, why is there so much hate? Why are people buying the tin foil ice cream? And third, why do you appeal to the broad range of human experience when it comes to love and hate yet feel free to reject the broad range of human experience in its denial of atheism?

I am genuinely interested to hear your explanation of your double standard when it comes to Christians and Jains. And I would really like to hear how you bridge the gap between nervous systems (where *all* pain and pleasure is experienced) without resorting to the market of collective choices (which has no pain or pleasure). And even if you get to the market, this reduces all questions of morality to a matter of consumer choice. And how is that morality?

CHAPTER 5

THE GREAT JACUZZI OF CONSUMERISM

Your next section is comparatively short, and this response will also be. In "Doing Good for God," you grant that Christians have often done good in the world, but that they have been restricted by their dogmas, which have greatly hampered them. In contrast to this, you hold forth the far better example of secular philanthropists, who are untrammeled by any restrictive doctrines. For an example of the former, you admire Mother Teresa (*kind* of), but then say that she was encumbered by the heavy weight of her dogmatic religious convictions.

Here we Christians are distracted by issues like abortion when there are all these other situations we could be doing something about.

> At this very moment, millions of sentient people are suffering unimaginable physical and mental afflictions, in circumstances where the compassion of God is nowhere to be seen, and the compassion of human beings is often hobbled by preposterous ideas about sin and salvation. (37)

Every time you speak this way, I want to bring you back to the fundamental question about suffering. Given your principles, what is wrong with it? If I am living here in North America and my nervous system is not wired up to those who are suffering in Africa, why, given your principles, should I care? If ten people die in agony on the other side of the world, or if ten million do, if the word never gets to me, and the pain never registers in me, then why should I care?

Don't get me wrong. I believe we *must* care . . . because we are all created in the image of God, and Christ died for all the nations of men. But you would call this just one of my silly superstitions. Christ told us that we were to take the gospel to every creature, and this includes those cultural blessings that the gospel brings with it. But that's what *I* think. I am asking *you* why pain that never registers as pain *in me* brings any moral obligation to me. In addition, if I am living here in North America, that great Jacuzzi of consumerism, and enjoying the heck out of it, then why should I surrender all that in order to go suffer through what it takes to bring some relief to others? Who cares? Before I cared, no pain in me. After I cared, lots of pain in me. Please explain to me why I should exchange pleasure for pain in the only place where pleasure and pain register. Why are pleasure and absence of suffering the highest good? And if they *are* the highest good, then how can we possibly get to a collective morality when human societies don't have nerve endings?

You are assuming a great solidarity of nervous systems, and I do not see how collective moral obligation can arise out of this—particularly since the pain and pleasure calculus you use does not jump from one nervous system to another. On top of that, what gives pleasure to certain subgroups of human nervous systems gives pain to other subgroups. How are we to sort this out? If pain and pleasure are the real things that count, it would seem that we have to side with the bigger tribe because they are carrying around more nerve endings. They would, collectively, experience more pleasure, and the defeated tribe would experience less pain. And after the genocide, the defeated tribe would experience *no* pain. So as far as the atheist is concerned, that problem is permanently solved, and we have ourselves a final solution. I know that you are appalled by this kind of reasoning and say that it does not represent your thinking, which I grant. But I want to know *why* it does not represent your thinking. Why do you assume a solidarity of all humankind as opposed to a tribal or racial solidarity? To what objective standard to you appeal for your code of conduct?

One other brief comment. You point out that many abortions occur naturally, and you draw a rather strange inference from it. "There is an obvious truth here that cries out for acknowledgment: if God exists, He is the most prolific abortionist of all" (38). You do not appear to understand that if God is the giver of life (and He is), He may also take that life away. We bless the name of the Lord. We may not take life away on our own authority precisely because we did not give it in the first place. God, "if He exists," does not have to fill out a police report down at the station every time someone dies of a heart attack. God is not guilty of negligent manslaughter because he let a man eat way too many Krispy Kremes.

CHAPTER 6

ANY REASON HE SHOULD?

Your next section asks the question, "Are Atheists Evil?" Your argument here rests upon a common misunderstanding of a standard Christian argument, and so I am grateful for the opportunity to sort this out. In short, the issue is not whether atheists are evil, but rather, given atheism, what possible definition can we find for evil. The argument is not one about personal character but rather about what the tenets of atheism logically entail.

But there is another wrinkle as well. The Christian position is not that atheists are sinners, but rather that *people* are sinners. Consequently, when *any* false ideology (atheistic or theistic) gets hold of a collective group of people, we are bound to find there are no brakes to restrain the natural sinful tendencies of the people involved. This will of course manifest itself in different ways according to the differences of the ideologies. It explains why nations that are formally atheistic are awful (and dangerous) places to live. But at the same time, we could all rattle off false theistic ideologies that turned the places they controlled into hellholes. This just means that men sin in different ways.

So all this happens because people are sinners—and the Christian faith accounts for the reality and influence of this sin. *Theistic* rulers of Israel put Jesus to death, and this is obviously something that Christians condemn. Theistic Christian societies in the medieval period exhibited murderous behavior toward Jews, and this too is something that any Christian with an open Bible would have to condemn. Mao murdered his millions in the grip of his atheistic ideology, and we stand against that as well. It is not that theistic totalitarians are okay with us and atheistic totalitarianism is not. We reject it *all*, because God hates it all and will bring it into judgment at the last day. He is not going to wave through the pearly gates all the murderous thugs who did their evil in His name. Quite the reverse.

A quick comment on your comparisons of advanced societies (as the "least religious societies on earth") to the third worlders (bringing up the rear) which you identify as "unwaveringly religious." What you left out of that evaluation is what worldview was predominant in all the advanced countries you mention when they *first* attained that advanced position. All of the nations you mentioned (with the exception of Japan) were Christian at the time of their ascendancy. Not only so, but many of the nations you mention, having abandoned their Christian heritage, are also on their last legs. Europe, the remains of old Christendom, has about twenty years left before they go under the Islamic flood. In short, you have given us a picture of a cluster of prodigal sons, laughing in a tavern while spending their fathers' money and buying drinks for the house. But there is a difference between what it takes to make money and what it takes to spend it. The nations you mention became prosperous when they were under the strong influence of the Christian faith. They have abandoned that faith for the most part, and we shall now see how they will do. The checks are already starting to bounce.

Having made that point, let's return to the center of your argument. "If you are right to believe that religious faith offers the only real basis for morality, then atheists should be less moral than believers" (38–39). Again, the argument is not about the actual behavior of people. The argument is about what the actual behavior of people would be if they were logically consistent. As mentioned above, collective atheism tends toward that logical consistency, which is why I would oppose atheistic societies. But there is no reason to oppose, in the same way, an individual atheist who cannot see the logical outworkings of his own position. I am willing to cheerfully grant that there are many atheists that I would be happy to have live next door to me. I would be happy to ask them to watch my house while I was on vacation. I would not be compelled to think that as soon as we pulled around the corner, their atheism would compel them to run over and burn my house down.

Think of it this way. Let us suppose we have two men of atrocious character—they have both raped and murdered repeatedly and have expressed their contempt for the dignity of mankind in many other secret ways as well. They are both of them pieces of work, but one is a convinced atheist and the other is (in his intellectual commitments anyway) a Christian and a member of a Christian church. Now suppose further that because these two men are very clever, or because they were lucky enough to have incompetent cops assigned to their cases, or for whatever other reason, they both got away with their crimes, with no suspicion falling on either one of them. They both reached eighty years of age as respected members of their communities. Both of them successfully managed to live a double life. They have both come to their deathbeds, their crimes hidden and their intellectual commitments intact. One is still an atheist and the other still a Christian.

The first thinks to himself, "I made it through the obstacle course. I did whatever I wanted to do. I am about to die, and I will *never* have to answer for anything that I ever did." The second man is increasingly troubled in his conscience because "I got away with everything *here*, but I am going to a place where everything will be made manifest and judged." The former believes that he will not be judged for any of his crimes, and the second man believes that he will be judged for all of them. Now, given your atheism, which man is correct? This reveals that the wicked Christian lived an inconsistent life, while the wicked atheist lived a consistent life. His consistent lifestyle is not binding on you personally, but you are in no position to reject it for *him*.

Now my question is *not* "Aren't you a horrible criminal just like the first man?" The question is not whether or not you as an atheist are promoting the same criminal choices that this other atheist made for whatever reason. I am not like the Christian in this illustration, and there is no reason why you have to be like that atheist.

Rather, my question is simply this: having made those choices and congratulated himself on his deathbed, where is he wrong in his reasoning? I am not saying that his reasons provide a good rationale for you to go live that way—you obviously don't want to. But he *did* want to, and what in your thinking can persuade him to think differently? And the use of this phrase "want to" identifies where the problem is. Given atheism, morality reduces to personal preferences. You don't need to protest that you don't share *those* preferences. I grant it. But the man in my illustration doesn't share yours either. Any reason he should?

CHAPTER 7

GOD'S FAST BALL, HIGH AND INSIDE

The first part of your next section ("Who Puts the Good in the 'Good Book'?") is actually quite strong. You begin by noting that the point of truth is not our own personal convenience. "Even if atheism led straight to moral chaos, this would not suggest that the doctrine of Christianity is *true*" (46). In other words, the facts of the case never check with us first to see if their being true will put us out in any way. The square of the hypotenuse is what it is quite apart from my having indigestion over it. Two apples added to two apples will result in four apples however stern my letter to the editor might be. In short, truth is what it is. And thus far we for the most part agree.

But this is a two-edged point. I grant your central point about atheism—the fact that a truth leading straight to moral chaos does not make an opposing position true. But, as I said, this sentiment cuts both ways. The fact is that Christianity might lead straight to moral chaos, as *you* define it (after all, Christ came to turn father against son, and daughter against mother, and brought a sword instead of peace), and yet not be false.

The one word you use in the quote above that I might take issue with is the word *suggest*. If that word were *prove*, I would agree, but *suggest* is a good bit milder. If atheism leads to moral chaos, then would it not be wise to at least *check* some of the alternatives? Jesus taught this principle with regard to those who were considering what it meant to be His disciple, what it meant to follow Him. He told us to count the cost, and this means that there will be short-term costs to count. Hard consequences *suggest* that we ought to check our calculations more than once.

The difference between us is that the Christian knows that there will be short-term chaos but also knows that God has it under control and that "all things work together for good to them that love God, to them who are the called according to his purpose" (Rom. 8:28). The atheist who runs into moral chaos has arrived at his final home, given the truth of his premises. Nevertheless, we can agree on this at least— the truth is independent of our wishes and desires.

GOD'S FAST BALL, HIGH AND INSIDE   45

In the first part of this section, you rightly admonish liberal and moderate Christians for wanting to have it both ways. "God remains an absolute mystery, a mere source of consolation that is compatible with the most desolating evil" (48). You say that "liberal theology must stand revealed for what it is: the sheerest of mortal pretenses. The theology of wrath has far more intellectual merit" (48). In other words, the world is a screwed-up place, and *if* there is a God over it, then He cannot *just* be a comforter. The evil that exists in this world is here because God wills it, as everyone who believes in God must acknowledge at some level. He either wills it directly by His decrees (as I and my fellow Calvinists would say), or He wills it by allowing it to happen when He has the power to stop it (as other Christians hold). If some believers want to get away from this argument by appealing to something like free will, this only explains *why* God wills it. It does not alter, in the slightest, the *fact* that God willed it. So we agree here as well.

You used the example of the great Asian tsunami. We agree that, if there is a God, He did not find out about this disaster from CNN. He governs the earth, and this was something that happened on His watch. "Does disaster come to a city, unless the Lord has done it?" (Amos 3:6, ESV). So when you say that a "theology of wrath" has far more "intellectual merit," I agree. It is consistent with the facts. Those who are nicknamed

Calvinists do not have any unique problems with the "problem of evil." They just get more attention than other Christians on this point because they are willing to speak directly into the microphone. "Yes. God did this thing. And do you think that those on whom the tower fell were greater sinners? Unless you repent you will all likewise perish" (see Luke 13:5).

But it is not a theology only of wrath. Wrath is something that God invites us to flee from. And the only way to flee from the wrath of God is to flee *to* the wrath of God as exhibited on the cross where Jesus suffered, bled, and died. But God does tell us to flee from the wrath to come, which is only done through repentance and faith in Jesus Christ. He does not tell us to flee from the doctrine of wrath in sophisticated embarrassment. But I want to take this a step further. You are exactly right that *all* Christians, if they are to be intellectually honest, must acknowledge that God is the ultimate governor of earthquakes, tsunamis, hurricanes, genocides, and wars. This creates the "problem of evil" for us. How can a God who is infinitely just, kind, merciful, and loving (which we Christians also affirm) be the same one who unleashes these terrible "acts of God"? It is a good question, but it is one that can only be answered by embracing the problem. We solve the problem of evil by kissing the rod and the hand that wields it.

This sounds outrageous to you, I know, but it is the only way to genuinely deal with the problem of evil. It is either the problem of evil, which the Christian has, or "Evil? No problem!" which the atheist has. Consider the tsunami from *your* premises. You spoke of the day "one hundred thousand children were simultaneously torn from their mother's arms and casually drowned" (48). Now I can only understand you being indignant with God over this if He is really *there*. But what if He is *not* there? What follows then? This event had no more ultimate significance than a solar flare or a virus going extinct or a desolate asteroid colliding with another asteroid or the gradual loss of Alabama to kudzu or me scratching my head just now. These are just atoms banging around. This is what they do.

It is very clear from how you write that you do not believe that God is there and that you are also very angry with Him for not being there. Many of these people who were drowned were no doubt praying before they died. You throw that fact at us believers (which you can do, because, believing in God, we do have a problem of evil). But if we throw it back to you, what must *you* say about the tsunami and its effects? It was a natural event driven by natural causes and has to be seen as an integral part of the natural order of things. There was absolutely *nothing* wrong with it. These things happen. Take the words of appalling comfort that John Lennon wrote for us.

Imagine there's no heaven
It's easy if you try
No hell below us
Above us only sky
Imagine all the people living for today

But they are not living for today, not anymore. Their bloated bodies are "dragged from the sea" (48). When their bodies are lined up on the beach, you want to rage, but there is no object for your anger. There is no wall to punch. Because above you *and them* is "only sky." You want to rail against God, but He is not there. *But that means He didn't do it.* So who did? There is no who. Only sky above us and only dirt below. In short, you have no right to exhibit the slightest bit of indignation over "the neglect" that is being shown to these particular end products of mindless evolution. There is no neglect. Nature eats her own and will do so until every last sun has gone out. Deal with it.

You may want to turn this around and pretend that I say these things because I am calloused. Not a bit of it. I am a Christian, and I know that death and evil and disasters are all enemies. We are not without natural affection. Pure religion visits widows and orphans in their affliction (James 1:27). True religion is surprised at the last day to discover that God remembers all the acts of kindness done, down to the last drink of cold water (Matt. 25:34–40). True religion will ask, "Lord, when did we do these things for you?" And He will *reply*. As Francis Schaeffer memorably put it, "He is there, and He is not silent."

When we look at the horrific things that happen in this world, there really are only two options: either these things have a larger purpose, or they do not. If they do, then they will tie into that larger purpose at some point under the mastery of God, and all manner of things shall be well. This is the deeply comedic vision for the world that the Christian faith offers and which Peter Leithart describes so well in his book *Deep Comedy*.[4] But if they have no larger purpose, then there is nothing wrong with them *now*, just the way they are. If the two of us were looking at a news report of the latest atrocity, I would say that at some point in the future, in some fundamental way, that will be *put right*. You want to say, as an atheist, that it will not ever be put right. But you refuse, for some reason, to take the next logical step and admit that there is therefore nothing wrong with it now. I will say more about this inconsistency in a future section.

One more thing. You say,

> You are using your own moral intuitions to authenti-
> cate the wisdom of the Bible—and then, in the next
> moment, you assert that we human beings cannot
> possibly rely upon our own intuitions to rightly guide
> us in the world; rather, we must depend upon the
> prescriptions of the Bible. You are using your own

---

4. Peter Leithart, *Deep Comedy* (Moscow, ID: Canon Press, 2006).

moral intuitions to decide that the Bible is the appropriate guarantor of your moral intuitions. Your own intuitions are still primary, and your reasoning is circular. *We* decide what is good in the Good Book. (49)

This criticism would apply to those who come to the Bible to cherry-pick their inspirational verses. But I do not see how it applies to those who are willing to accept the Bible as it comes and who are willing to learn how to submit to the discipline of thinking scripturally across the board. Lots of people *do* project their middle-class values onto the Bible and skate right over the embarrassing parts. But how would you deal with biblical absolutists who are willing to take the Bible as God's fast ball, high and inside? I don't see how your critique would apply at all to those of us in that category.

For example, immediately after this point, you cite Deuteronomy 22:13–21 and say, "If we are civilized, we will reject this as the vilest lunacy imaginable" (50). I have argued from that passage before in my book on biblical courtship,[5] and I don't find this law of God's even a little bit shameful. I wouldn't dream of calling it "vile lunacy." So, what do you mean by "civilized"? Multiple questions arise. What does it mean to be civilized? Is it bad to be uncivilized? What are the standards of civilization, and who sets them? Why are those standards binding? Were the Aztecs civilized? How do civilizations arise? Did any great civilizations

---

5. Douglas Wilson, *Her Hand in Marriage* (Moscow, ID: Canon Press, 1997), pp. 24ff, 31.

ever arise by having a higher view of Deuteronomy than you currently do?

CHAPTER 8

KEROSENE THE WHOLE
ANT HILL

You then continue a point in your next section—with variations—that we have already discussed. But the more you press this point, the clearer the issues become. I am happy to go over this again because your additional comments set the problem up nicely.

I want to begin by noting the particular problem of this section. You have already chastised Christian believers over the problem of evil, and I have responded at that level. But here you present your atheism as a clear-sighted willingness to follow the argument all the way to the end, whatever the cost. But I have to admonish you here—you actually do nothing of the kind. Yours is *not* an atheism which rejects God and accepts all the consequences of that rejection regardless of how hard those consequences may be. Having rejected God, you remain a sentimentalist with your sentiments miraculously suspended in midair.

You pull out all the stops in presenting us with a particular instance of evil.

> Somewhere in the world a man has abducted a little girl. Soon he will rape, torture, and kill her. If an atrocity of this kind is not occurring at precisely this moment, it will happen in a few hours, or days at most . . . The same statistics also suggest that this girl's parents believe—as you believe—that an all-powerful and all-loving God is watching over them and their family. Are they right to believe this? Is it *good* that they believe this? No. The entirety of atheism is contained in this response. (50–51)

Well, depending on what you mean, no, it isn't. You do not go on to say that it is a matter of indifference whether or not they believe this. You think that it is *bad* that the parents believe this. But what does *bad* mean? By what standard? I have already shown that, given your premises, you have no grounds for denouncing the perpetrator of this horrific crime. Still less do you have grounds for denouncing the parents for not believing that the death of their little girl was ultimately senseless—as *you* would have them believe.

And this is where your sentimentalism kicks in with a vengeance. "An atheist is a person who believes that the murder of a single little girl—even once in a million years—casts doubt upon the idea of a benevolent God" (52). This is not even close. Why do you halt between two opinions? Atheism not only casts doubt upon the idea of a benevolent God (which it certainly does), *but it also destroys the very concept of benevolence itself.* Benevolence is simply a chemical reaction that some organisms experience in their bone box. Other organisms (like the criminal organism that rapes and kills the little girl organism) don't have very much of it. But this is all just time and chance acting on matter. When you reject the triune God (in the name of benevolence!) I want to know what this all-authoritative benevolence actually is, by *your* accounting.

I do not believe that the indignation you display over these monstrosities is a sham. I believe that you truly feel this way. But then to pretend that these sentiments of yours are actually part of a courageous willingness to ask and answer the hard questions is a bit thick. There is no soundtrack to consistent atheism. No swelling violins in the background but rather stark, everlasting *silence*.

Many atheists *have* squarely faced the consequences of what they say they believe, but you do not even begin to approach this. And this is why your question to Christians is sad more than anything else. "Do you have the courage to admit the obvious?" (52). Oliver Wendell Holmes did. He knew what morality was, given the premises. Preferences with regard to morality were just that, *preferences*. Moral preferences are "more or less arbitrary."[6] Let that settle in your mind, without your fragments of atheistic sanctimony—emotional detritus left over from the previous Christian era. And let Holmes spell it out for you. "Do you like sugar in your coffee or don't you? . . . . So as to truth."[7] Or try this out: Truth is "the majority view of the nation which can lick all others."[8] And rights are "what a given crowd will fight for."[9]

If the material universe is what you claim, then you need to embrace the ramifications of what you claim. The wiping out of a nation or a city does not have the significance that you are unsuccessfully trying to create for it. Holmes again: "I doubt if a shudder would go through the spheres if the whole ant heap were kerosened."[10] Your ideas are nothing but epiphenomena in that curious chemical vat of yours that we are pleased to call a brain. But let Holmes point out the comparative value of one part of your body over another. "I wonder if cosmically an idea is any more important than the bowels."[11] Now not even Holmes is fully

---

6. Albert Alschuler, *Law Without Values* (Chicago: University of Chicago Press, 2000), 1.

7. Alschuler., 1.

8. Ibid., 11.

9. Ibid., 6.

10. Ibid., 23.

11. Ibid., p. 23.

KEROSENE THE WHOLE ANT HILL   57

consistent with his premises, because if that thought
of his were correct, then all thoughts are on the same
level as a bowel movement, and that would include
this particular thought of *his*, which would give us full
liberty to ignore him. But although Holmes pulls up
short before tumbling into the abyss, he is certainly
willing to affirm far more of what is necessarily en-
tailed in his atheism than you are. He is well down the
road; you are still in the driveway.

> Once you stop swaddling the reality of the world's
> suffering in religious fantasies, you will feel in your
> bones just how precious life is—and, indeed, how
> unfortunate it is that millions of human beings suffer
> the most harrowing abridgements of their happiness
> for no good reason at all. (54)

But there have been many clear-sighted atheists who
have preceded you who have felt nothing of the kind in
their bones. And they can explain to you clearly why,
if there is nothing above us but sky, certain things
follow. Your sentimental atheism is a hodgepodge of
Christian leftovers.

You ask, "What was God doing while Katrina laid
waste to their city?" (52). Well, to give the biblical answer, during Katrina, God was laying waste to the city.
This is something even insurance companies know; it
was an act of God. He is not an absentee deity; scriptural Christians do not feel in the least bit apologetic
about how God governs the world. What He did to

New Orleans was holy, righteous, just, and good. Some of it may have been an obvious chastisement for those who would build a major city below sea level in hurricane country and then attempt to govern it through corruption and vice.

Some of God's goodness was apparent on the face of it at the time, and some of the righteousness behind His action will not be apparent until the Last Day. But there is no blemish at all in God's ways with man. We believe by faith that God draws straight with crooked lines. You are free to reject this, as you clearly have. But when you reject it, you must acknowledge that you have *also* lost the very concept of a crooked line. And it follows that you must stop being indignant about these nonexistent crooked lines.

Unaware of all this, you state the problem of evil in its classic form.

> This is the age-old problem of theodicy, of course, and we should consider it solved. If God exists, either He can do nothing to stop the most egregious calamities, or He does not care to. God, therefore, is either impotent or evil. (55)

Yes, this is the problem of evil, and it is the question that every Christian theist must answer. Since the idea of divine impotence in effect ungods God, not many of us have taken this route. But in this effeminate age, some professing Christians are now trying it, and they call their explanation the "openness of God." God troubleshoots as we go, but He actually does not do it very well. In this view, God reacts to disasters as they happen, but His reflexes are pretty poor. He runs after disasters, wringing His hands. In this view, God is a lot like FEMA—unprepared, incompetent, disorganized, and two weeks late.

The other option is that God does not want to stop the evil just now. If He wanted to stop it, He would have. This is exactly right. But we believe, beyond just this raw statement, that God has *glorious* reasons for this unwillingness to intervene. Those glorious reasons will be made manifest on the day when every mouth will be stopped, and every tongue confesses that all His actions throughout all history were good and true. Until that day, we take it on faith.

You say that you cannot accept this. You don't have that faith. Fair enough. But you must know that this means that you *also* do not have the faith to believe that there are such things as benevolence, kindness, mercy, and love. Either mercy is genuine and real, and the tension along with the existence of genuine evil requires faith in the triune God of the Bible, or we reject that tension—and the reality of mercy and evil along with it. What you call mercy is nothing more than what happens when you pour vinegar into the baking soda. When we look at a fourth grader's science fair project, it does not occur to us to pronounce that his papier-mâché volcano is speaking profound truths or exhibiting great philanthropy. If this is what you want to claim, then go right ahead. And if you do, we won't listen because the next book you write (just like the previous ones) is just the smoke from the chemical reaction down in the hole. But if you don't want to claim it, then you need to drop everything and spend some time searching for your god. For in that case nothing would be more apparent than the fact that you *have* one and you are no atheist at all.

"It is terrible that we all die and lose everything we love; it is doubly terrible that so many human beings suffer needlessly while alive" (56–57). And this is my point. In your view, all suffering is (by definition) senseless. It is not immediately needless, given the evolutionary struggle that you say is occurring, but in the larger view of things, it is meaningless. And since evolution is not anything that anybody actually requested, I guess it is needless at that level also. The Holocaust is on the same level as boys pouring kerosene in the ant hill, just for fun and just because they can. The Christian is the one saying that all this will eventually be put right. You are the one saying it *cannot* be put right and, by unacknowledged implication, that there is nothing wrong with it now.

Ironically, after unwittingly marshaling all these inconsistencies, you then say that "criticism of religious faith [is] a moral and intellectual necessity" (57). All right, then, criticize away. Assemble the ants to complain about the boulder that rolled down the hill and destroyed their prosperous city. Circulate a petition. File that indignant petition with the authorities . . . wait. There are no authorities. Above the outraged ants, only sky. Nobody is in charge of this. Nobody did it. Shit happens.

CHAPTER 9

ALL OVER TARNATION

I n your next section, "The Power of Prophecy," we move from the "great" questions like the problem of evil to some particular and specific questions you raise about the Bible.

You say that Christians argue that "many of the ideas recounted in the New Testament confirm Old Testament prophecy" (57). A better way of putting it is that we believe many of the predictions made in the Old Testament of the coming Messiah were fulfilled in the New, but your expression of it is certainly fair enough. But you then go on to claim that it would be really easy to rig this kind of fulfillment. "Wouldn't it have been within the power of any mortal to write a book that confirms the predictions of a previous book?" (57) Well, in the abstract that would be very easy to do. But you are leaving out of your reckoning the fact that the Christian faith was first preached and established in the face of stiff opposition. You are not the first debunker that the Christian faith has ever encountered. This means that when the disciples wrote their gospel accounts of Christ's life, they were doing so in a hostile environment in which any attempt to be cute with the known facts would be immediately turned against them. It is in this setting that we should take note of the prophecies of Christ's birthplace in Bethlehem (a hard event to stage), the betrayal price that Judas took, the details of Christ's passion, and, most important, the predictions of His resurrection. Coming back from the dead after three days in the tomb is notoriously hard to rig. As the apostle Paul once put it, "These things were not done in a corner" (Acts 26:26). Everybody was watching what was happening, friend and foe alike. After-the-fact prophecy fulfillment is not hard in a vacuum, but it would have been hard in the circumstances in which the Christian faith first took root.

Some of your other objections do not go very deep, and so I don't think I need to spend a lot of time with them. For example, you point to the prophecy in Isaiah about a virgin conceiving and giving birth to a son who will be named "God with us," and you rightly note that the Hebrew word *alma* means virgin *or* young woman. This is quite correct. Isaiah is giving a double prophecy here—a young woman in his day would conceive (as a sign to Ahaz) and a virgin would conceive a child sometime in the future. This is a double prophecy which is allowed for in the Hebrew. But we can see that something is up in the Greek translation of this passage in the Septuagint. This translation was done centuries after Isaiah and long before the advent of Christ. No Christians had anything to do with it, and these Old-Testament-era Jews translated *alma* into Greek as *parthenos,* which can *only* mean virgin. The expectation of the Jews prior to Christ included an expectation of a virgin birth.

So this is how I would answer your assertion that *virgin* was a Christian mistranslation. "It seems all but certain that the dogma of the virgin birth, and much of the Christian world's resulting anxiety about sex, was a product of a mistranslation from the Hebrew" (58). As to your assertion that Christians have a deep-seated anxiety over sex, I would counter by suggesting that for *real* sexual angst, you would have to try someplace like Manhattan. Looking around at church here in Idaho and judging from all the kids being born into the congregation, it would seem to me that a bunch of Christians didn't get the memo.

You also bring up a problem with how the biblical writers arranged their footnotes, calling this an error of scholarship. "And the evangelists made other errors

of scholarship. Matthew 27:9–10, for instance, claims
to fulfill a saying that it attributes to Jeremiah. The
saying actually appears in Zechariah 11:12–13" (58).
But what you fail to take into account here is the fact
that it was a custom among the Jews, when referring
to *two* sources, to have the attribution go to the major prophet, which in this case was Jeremiah. Jeremiah
does give a prophecy that in the future of Israel fields
will be bought for silver (Jer. 32:9), and Zechariah's
prophecy is more specific, mentioning the amount
that Judas would receive (Zech. 11:12-13). Matthew
is referring to both, quotes one, and gives the credit, according to their custom, to the major prophet.
Your objection here actually amounts to saying that
Matthew should have followed *The Chicago Manual
of Style*. But it would be just as valid for Matthew to
claim that you had cited a source incorrectly because
you wrote *Ibid.* in one of your footnotes. "I looked and
looked," Matthew said, "and there is no book in the
whole library called *Ibid.*" On another front, you complain that the Bible doesn't really treat some of the
subjects you would have preferred.

> A book written by an omniscient being could con-
> tain a chapter on mathematics that, after two thou-
> sand years of continuous use, would still be the
> richest source of mathematical insight humanity
> has ever known. Instead, the Bible contains no for-
> mal discussion of mathematics and some obvious
> mathematical errors . . . (60)

Well, the first part of this is right, in a weird kind of way, but a complaint of this nature amounts to an unwillingness to let God be God and tell us what He would like us to know and to do so in a way that reveals what *He* believes to be important. We have no mathematical books in the Bible—to take an extreme example of what I am saying here—for the same reason that God did not include the perfect *Star Trek* novella in there. Mathematics as a subject is just fine, and God thought it was cool enough to embed it in everything He made, but it is not nearly as important in the communication of divine truth as poetry is. We can tell this by looking at how God actually speaks to us. Your preference for mathematics over poetry evidences a marked Hellenistic bias over the Hebraic mind. But there is no *a priori* reason why we should think that mathematics is capable of doing for us what the Scriptures (as they actually are) do for us.

But even though mathematics does not warrant a separate book of its own in the Bible, this is no reason for asserting that Scripture contains mathematical errors. As an example of one of the "obvious mathematical errors," you cite 1 Kings 7:23–26 and 2 Chronicles 4:2–5, which you say state that "the ratio of the circumference of a circle to its diameter" is three to one. This, you say, is "not impressive" (61). But these passages say nothing of the kind. The Scriptures are not telling us the value of *pi*. They are not talking about "a circle" in the abstract. They are talking about the bronze laver or "sea" that Solomon had ordered to be cast. This is a measurement of an actual bronze laver in the real world, and in that world, unlike the pristine world of Euclid, the line of the circumference has an actual *thickness*. The laver was not made out of a paper-thin sheet of bronze.

You are suggesting that if Euclid had been able to visit Solomon for a little geometry workshop, that Solomon would have been scratching his head over Euclid's insistence that Solomon not be allowed to build a laver with a circumference of thirty cubits and a diameter of ten cubits.

"But I want to," Solomon would say. "Well, you can't," Euclid fired back.

"What shall I do with the one we already have?" "I'm sorry, you don't have one. It's not possible," Euclid said.

"What's not possible," Solomon said, "is a laver made out of mathematical points. We tried that. It leaked all over tarnation."

CHAPTER 10

WHAT COLOR ARE YOUR ARGUMENTS?

Your next section, "The Clash of Science and Religion," begins by taking issue with the National Academy of Sciences. Among other things, that august academy said, "'Science can say nothing about the supernatural. Whether God exists or not is a question about which science is neutral'" (63). You took issue with this because, as you put it, "The truth, however, is that the conflict between religion and science is unavoidable" (63).

Now I need to say at the outset that I *agree* with you that there is a necessary clash between "neutral" science and religion. This is because I believe that there is no such thing as neutrality anywhere. If there is a triune God, and if Jesus Christ is His only begotten Son, then this divine being is not confined in anything as tiny as the "supernatural." Jesus Christ is Lord of all, or He is not Lord at all. This means that He is the Lord of all science. We both reject the truce offered by the National Academy of Sciences, but for different reasons. I reject it because I believe the lordship of Christ swallows up so-called scientific neutrality. You reject it because, in effect, what you will accept as reasonable evidence swallows up all claims to truth that fall outside the definitions you have set.

But having said this, how you go about defining science is truly curious. You say, "The core of science is not controlled experiment or mathematical modeling; it is intellectual honesty" (64). You do this to allow for historical claims to be lumped under science—the example you used is the fact that the Japanese bombed Pearl Harbor in 1941. Anything that is intellectually honest is science; anything that is intellectually dishonest is not. Okay. Now who is in charge of determining this? The National Academy of Intellectual Honesty?

You say something similar here:

> It is time we acknowledged a basic feature of human discourse: when considering the truth of a proposition, one is either engaged in an honest appraisal of the evidence and logical arguments, or one isn't. Religion is the one area of our lives where people

imagine that some other standard of intellectual integrity applies. (64–65)

Now you have already allowed that historical claims are, in principle, scientific claims, provided they are made by men and women who are intellectually honest. So what do you do with the claim that Jesus rose from the dead? Christians claim that this happened in history, not in a transcendent supernatural realm. We claim it took place in Jerusalem. According to Scripture, and according to the basic Christian confession of the Creed, it occurred "under Pontius Pilate." Now this is a historical claim, straight up the middle, pure and simple. You said, in the quote above, that intellectual honesty will engage in "an honest appraisal of the evidence." What does this look like when we Christians are making our scientific claim (according to your unique definition) about the raising of Jesus from the dead? Do you go check the empty tomb? Is that part of an honest appraisal of the evidence? Or do you have an *a priori* assumption that such a thing cannot happen because it has never happened before? And because of that assumption do you refuse to look at the evidence? Who is being intellectually honest in such a circumstance—the person who runs to the tomb, like Peter, or the one who doesn't?

We *understand* the person who doesn't bother even to check a story like this, but of course, we would understand him equally well if a couple of goofball time-travelers from the twenty-first century showed up in first-century Palestine with a DVD and a plasma television set (and a portable generator). They set up a little theater on the south side of the city and invite everyone to come see *Pride and Prejudice* (with subtitles in Aramaic). Now is the person who refuses to come look at this fraud (or display of demonism, take your choice) being scientific or not? According to your new definition of science, anyone who refused to check out these things known to him to be thundering impossibilities (but which are known to *us* to be common and everyday sorts of things) is being intellectually dishonest. But this seems a bit harsh. After all, imagine trying to explain (to someone like George Washington) your handheld calculator, your laptop, the internet, your cell phone, nuclear reactors, your handheld device, and your pickup truck. But if enough people that he trusted said, "Come, *see* . . .," he might be persuaded to come and see. And what if he saw? Suppose you are Washington's hard-bitten cynical friend who refused to go with him. And when he came back, you still refused to believe him because of your *a priori* assumptions about what was and was not possible? Is that science?

You say, "The conflict between science and religion is reducible to a simple fact of human cognition and discourse: either a person has good reasons for what he believes or he does not" (66–67). Did Peter, having seen the risen Lord, have good reason for believing in the resurrection? You would say that *if* he did see Him, then he would have good reason, but he didn't see him because he *couldn't* have seen him. But you are saying this on the basis of an *a priori* assumption about the universe, and not on the basis of how we normally go about establishing historical claims, which is by means of weighing eyewitness accounts. If you had an *a priori* assumption that you lived in a universe in which Japanese attacks on Pearl Harbor were an impossibility, well then, when the witnesses start showing up with their crazy stories, you know just what to do.

You then say something else that is curious. "Everyone recognizes that to rely upon 'faith' to decide specific questions of historical fact is ridiculous" (67). Well, this is strange. Peter and James and John didn't rely on faith to determine that Jesus rose. They relied on their eyes and hands. And Thomas was the most empirical of them all. He wouldn't believe unless he actually saw and touched the risen Jesus. There it is—real-life science in action and in the Bible! They confirmed that He rose the same way they confirmed everything else that happened in their lives. And for those of us who did *not* see the risen Jesus, we rely on their eyewitness testimony. I did not see the Lord's resurrection, the battle of Waterloo, the great fire of London, or George Washington's crossing of the Delaware. But I believe that all of them happened, and

I do so for the same exact reason. I find the eyewitness testimony that has come down to us concerning these events to be credible. Why am I intellectually dishonest for believing the first item on this list, but not for believing the remaining three? You would say it is because a resurrection from the dead is a miracle, and miracles don't happen. But this is your materialist faith kicking in again. This is a mere assumption of yours.

And speaking of your materialist *faith*, here is something else that you say. "It is time that we admitted that faith is nothing more than the license religious people give one another to keep believing when reasons fail" (67). It is clear from what we have discussed that you have faith also—faith that the universe is a closed system and that something like a resurrection is inconceivable. But this is not something you discovered by looking into a microscope. It is a philosophical axiom of yours—it is an article of *faith*. And, as we have just learned, faith is nothing more than "the license that atheists give one another to keep on not believing when reasons press in on them."

You say: "Religion is the one area of our discourse where it is considered noble to pretend to be certain about things no human being could possibly be certain about" (67). You are certain that Peter did not see Jesus when He rose from the dead. But this certainty of yours arises from your convictions about the nature

WHAT COLOR ARE YOUR ARGUMENTS? 75

of the universe, and not because you were in the room with Peter when he started talking to his invisible friend. Isn't that correct?

One last thing. The closed system that makes up your universe is impervious to any evidence to the contrary. Once grant that the world is this way, and anyone who comes bustling up to you with stories about men who came back from the dead is a *prima facie* nutjob. Simple. But you need to look at your closed-system universe again and look more closely at the price tag this time. Not only is this vast concourse of atoms spared the spectacle of a Jewish carpenter coming back from the grave, it is also spared *all* forms of immaterial realities. This would include, unfortunately, your arguments and thoughts. They are as immaterial as Farley's ghost. Show me your arguments for atheism under a microscope. Then I will think about believing them. What color are they? How much do they weigh? *What* are they made of?

CHAPTER 11

YOU TELL ME THAT IT'S EVOLUTION; WELL, YOU KNOW . . .

O f course, we were bound to get to the subject of evolution sooner or later. And this is unlikely to be the place where we both discover that we are "actually saying the same thing really." You think that creationists are bereft of any intellectual dignity whatever, and I agree with Malcolm Muggeridge that, in retrospect, evolution will be seen to have been one of the great jokes of history. Well, if your cavalry and ours are going to collide, we might as well do it at full gallop.

You maintain that evolution is a nailed-down fact, beyond all questioning. If someone does raise questions, this just demonstrates that he is a lunatic, and not that the question should have been raised. You say, in multiple ways, that evolution is "beyond all questioning." Well, here come some questions anyway.

"All complex life on earth has developed from simpler life-forms over billions of years. This is a fact that no longer admits of intelligent dispute" (68).

This sets the stage nicely. From this sentiment, I know that I am arguing with someone whose position is "what my net don't catch ain't fish," and that anyone who postulates that fish can be small enough to fit through a hole two inches square is an idiot. But here goes anyway. You begin by saying that the common use of the word *theory* does not detract from your case.

"Theories make predictions and can, in principle, be tested. The phrase "the theory of evolution" does not in the least suggest that evolution is not a fact" (69).

Your argument is that a theory is just a larger web of facts. A datum is a fact; a scientific theory is a cluster of facts, with no loss of facticity involved. Thus, for you, the theory of evolution is as factually settled as the germ theory of disease is.

So what should we call a "theory" that can still be falsified? Is relativity theory a fact? Will physicists five hundred years from now hold to the same identical theory . . . because it is an undisputed assemblage of *facts?* Thomas Kuhn was not talking about the theory of evolution in his book *The Structure of Scientific Revolutions*, but his description of how one paradigm passes from the stage and is replaced by another is an uncanny description of what is happening today to your beloved theory of evolution.[12] One of the telltale signs of trouble for a theory or a paradigm is when its defenders resort to name-calling in lieu of argument and obstinately defend an ossified orthodoxy instead of answering reasonable questions. And this is why science advances, as Max Planck observed, funeral by funeral. In passing, you try to deal with all the creationists who have somehow obtained advanced degrees in the hard sciences. "A handful of Christians appear to have done this; some have even obtained their degrees from reputable universities" (69). The first part of this is not quite accurate—a "handful"? My brother is one of these interlopers, and I can assure you that your minimized head counts reveal more than a little wishful thinking. You then deal with the problem with a little hand-waving sleight of definition. "While such people are technically 'scientists,' they are not behaving like scientists" (70). And why not? Well, they apparently disagree with *you*. Your field is philosophy and what you are doing here amounts to saying that anyone who is a Kantian, for example, can't be a *real* philosopher.

---

12. Thomas Kuhn, *The Structure of Scientific Revolutions* (Chicago: University of Chicago Press, 1962).

This is a sure indicator that an established position is in real trouble. Never, *ever*, engage. Just simply assert.

> We know that all complex organisms on earth, including ourselves, evolved from earlier organisms over the course of billions of years. The evidence for this is utterly overwhelming. (70)

Okay, could we who are numbered with the underwhelmed see some then? Can we talk about it? Will questions be allowed, or is this a "just have faith, my son" sort of religion?

But then, even in the midst of your assertions, you give the game away.

> There is no question that the diverse life we see around us is the expression of a genetic code written in the molecule DNA, that DNA undergoes chance mutations, and that some mutations increase an organism's odds of surviving and reproducing in a given environment. (70–71)

You get back on your evolutionary message in the second part of this quote—"chance mutations" and "increase odds." But look what you let slip in the first part. "There is no question that the diverse life we see around us is the expression of *a genetic code written . . .*" Exactly so—codes are *written*. A strand of DNA is a vast library. Scientists who have their satellite dishes pointed toward the sky in the hope of hearing from intelligent life out there know how to distinguish incoming messages from background noise. Otherwise, there would be no point. We know what information looks like, and we know what kind of source it comes from. This is because information is not made out of matter—rather it is matter that is organized in a particular way. If a scientist studying static from solar flare activity was to discover that all his printouts kept repeating the St. Crispin's Day speech from *Henry V*, his conclusion would *not* be that "given infinity and randomness, this was bound to happen sooner or later." And one strand of DNA is not just one speech from Shakespeare—it is the whole Folger Shakespeare Library.

But you persist in clinging to what you were taught by the priests in your youth.

> There is no question that human beings evolved from nonhuman ancestors. We know, from genetic evidence, that we share an ancestor with apes and monkeys, and that this ancestor in turn shared an ancestor with the bats and the flying lemurs. (71)

No question. No question. No *question*. Just keep saying that. But while we are on the subject, why did we decide to get rid of our uncanny sonar abilities? And since we are nothing but souped-up lemurs, let me raise (*again*) the question of the trustworthiness of our thought processes. Let us assume that evolution is not done with us, and we keep on advancing through the fog. When we have evolved for ten million more years, and our distant descendants look back on us,

will they think of our current cogitations and philoso-
phies as barely distinguishable from lemur-thought? If
not, then how is that evolution? If so, why should we
trust *anything* that we are currently thinking?

You felt, obviously, the need to take on the critics
of evolution who are found in the Intelligent Design
movement. But, not surprisingly, you are dismissive,
and you do not really take them on at all. According
to you, ID is "nothing more than a program of political and religious advocacy masquerading as science"
(72). The way you try to engage with them, however,
shows that you are grossly unacquainted with the lit-
erature. "The argument runs more or less like this: everything that exists has a cause . . ." (72). You are trying to summarize the arguments of the contemporary
Intelligent Design movement, and what you actually
do is haul out an argument from the medieval theo-
logian Thomas Aquinas. But the characteristic arguments of ID involve concepts like information theory
and irreducible complexity. From your summary, it is
pretty clear that you have not read any of the ID stuff.
Why are you going into print on it? This nagging suspicion is clinched with this observation of yours.

"Even if we accepted that the universe simply had to
be designed by a designer, this would not suggest that
this designer is the biblical God or that He approves of
Christianity" (73).

Here you are trying to argue against ID by employing one of the arguments *that they themselves make*. ID advocates will tell you that their arguments do not prove the existence of God and are not intended to. That is one of the problems that I as a Christian have with the ID movement. I really appreciate the demolition job they are doing on Darwin, but I think they should drive their truck a lot further down the road and then unload the whole thing. A variation of the "infinite regress" (73) argument that you make is an argument that I have presented before to a friend of mine in the ID movement. But the reason I bring this up is that what this proves is that you are interacting with a movement and you have not taken the trouble to read (or at least remember) some of their basic arguments. Before you set up shop to dismiss the ID arguments, you should at least ascertain what they are.

Just one more point, and then I am done. You say: "The biologist J.B.S. Haldane is reported to have said that, if there is a God, He has 'an inordinate fondness for beetles.' One would have hoped that an observation this devastating would have closed the book on creationism for all time" (75–76). There are, as you point out, over 350,000 *species* of beetles. But why this should count as an argument against the triune God of Scripture, I surely don't know. I am a die-hard creationist, and I think it is the coolest thing in the world that our God created that many different kinds of beetles. What this really means is the God of Scripture is not the tidy god of Plato that philosophers prefer to believe (or disbelieve) in. I am a *Christian*; I love it when our God misbehaves like this.

CHAPTER 12

LET THE DIALOGUE BEGIN!

Your next to last section is entitled "Religion, Violence, and the Future of Civilization" but it could just as easily be named after Richard Weaver's famous book, *Ideas Have Consequences*. As you say, "The truth is, it really matters what billions of human beings believe and why they believe it" (87). I actually agreed with a number of things you said in this section but was troubled by the fact that you are trying to build a solid house on such a shaky foundation.

For example, you begin by saying, "Unfortunately, there are many books that pretend to divine authorship, and they make incompatible claims about how we all must live" (79). Well, sure. I agree with that. The Koran and the Bible, to take just two examples, cannot both be the Word of God. But how is this observation an argument against the concept of divine revelation? If there are a million dollars just sitting there, and somewhere out there is a long-lost heir, it is in the highest degree likely that many will show up claiming to be that heir. Nobody counterfeits brown shopping bags, but they do counterfeit twenty-dollar bills. To argue from numerous false claimants to the conclusion that there must not be an inheritance is a dubious procedure. To argue that there is no such thing as the Federal Reserve because of a rise in counterfeiting is not a structurally sound argument. When you have rival claims about ultimate reality, one of the things that you must do is sort them out.

You point out that our culture has grown hypersensitive about religious issues. "Our fear of provoking religious hatred has rendered us unwilling to criticize ideas that are increasingly maladaptive and patently ridiculous" (80). This is a good observation, but this is something that your secularism has done for us and all in the interest of building up mutual toleration and group hugs for everyone. And so, I would ask you, point blank, are you having second thoughts about secular liberalism? Do you believe that we should have a line on the form that immigrants must fill out that asks them if they think Allah is the one true God, and whether Mohammed is his prophet?

You also observe, again rightly, that

religion raises the stakes of human conflict much higher than tribalism, racism, or politics ever can, as it is the only form of in-group/out-group thinking that casts the differences between people in terms of eternal rewards and punishments. (80)

Then you say that "one of the enduring pathologies of human culture is the tendency to raise children to fear and demonize other human beings on the basis of religious faith" (80). You are talking here about people in one religion despising members of another religion—but the same thing could be said about people despising others for even having a religion at all. For example, I recently read a book in which the author wrote that people who believe in God are deranged. Okay, I'm trying to be a little cute here . . . the book was yours. "It is not at all clear how we should proceed in our dialogue with the Muslim world, but deluding ourselves with euphemisms is not the answer" (85). You go on to say that "most Muslims are *utterly deranged by their religious faith*" (85, emphasis yours). After this, you add, "It seems profoundly unlikely that we will heal the divisions in our world through interfaith dialogue" (86). Well, yeah. Especially *that* kind of interfaith dialogue, "you idiot."

I believe that Islam is a false religion, and I believe that the people who adhere to it are deluded. I believe that they are objectively wrong, and that the Christian faith is objectively right. But I believe that Muslims are men and women created in the image of God, fallen in sin, and potential recipients of the offered gospel of forgiveness in Christ. You say that we ought to move away from politically correct euphemisms (which I agree with), and then to go on to say that everyone in the history of the world outside your little atheistic society is a raving psychopathic wackjob. "Let the dialogue begin!"

You give a long list of animosities, and say, *rightly*, that they "are often the products of their religious identities" (81). But again, for Christians, this is beside the point. We don't believe that religion is the answer. We believe Christ is the answer. When you combine religion with sinners, what you get is religious sin. And when you combine serious religion with sinners, what you get is *serious* religious sin. All this does is confirm one of the basic tenets of the Christian faith, which is that the human race is all screwed up.

At a number of points in this section, you turn your critique on your fellow secularists, pointing out that they have been a little naive. "And yet, while the religious divisions in our world are self-evident, many people still imagine that religious conflict is always caused by a lack of education, by poverty, or by politics" (82). You go on to add that "jihadist violence is not merely a matter of education, poverty, or politics" (83). This is exactly right. The problem of sin cannot be removed by education, money, or getting a bill through Congress. But neither can it be solved by getting rid of religion. All that does is give you a *secular* religion of the kind currently on tap in North Korea. The problem is not found in abstract nouns—like religion, education, wealth, etc. Neither is the solution to be found there. The problem is in concrete persons. People are sinful, and they want to throw rocks at one another. Put them down in one place and the rocks they throw will be basalt; in another region they will throw granite. But they will throw *something*. If we are to solve the problems you point out in this section, something must be done with the people. I will say something about this in my last section.

In the meantime, "Western secularists, liberals, and moderates have been very slow to understand this. The cause of their confusion is simple: they don't know what it is like to *really* believe in God" (83). But again, from a Christian perspective there is obviously no problem with really believing in God. The problem is really believing in God in such a way that neither accounts for nor solves the basic sin problem of the human heart, but leaves it untouched.

You point out that Europe is in grave danger of being overrun by Islam, and everyone agrees with you here. You say, "The birth rate among European Muslims is three times that of their non-Muslim neighbors" (83). You lament the fact that the only voices raised in warning against this problem are those of fascists. Actually, many Christians are talking about this

problem also, but from your book it appears that joining with Christians to do something about this would
be as detestable to you as joining with the fascists.
Nevertheless, the problem isn't going away. "France
will be a majority-Muslim country in twenty-five
years—and that is if immigration were to stop tomorrow" (83–84).

And this leaves you with a real dilemma. You want
to save the secular democracies of Europe. You want
to do it without religion. But secularism, which has
apparently taken to worshiping the condom, produces
low birth rates and is consequently in mortal danger
of being overrun within the next twenty years. Ideas
do have consequences. And what does Darwin—one of
the framers of your ideas—say about one population
replacing another?

CHAPTER 13

THE ULTIMATE STORY

I hope you have taken the time to read through this short response to your small book. Whether you have or not, I do not regret taking the time to compose it—your writings on this subject are certainly widespread, and this response has enabled me to speak not only to you, but to anyone interested in the other side of the story.

In this last section, I want to do two things. The first is to briefly address some of the comments you made in your conclusion. The second is to simply make a brief statement of the Christian faith in the context of our discussion.

In a previous section, I said that you were trying to function as a sentimental atheist. To echo the famous words of C.S. Lewis, you "remove the organ and demand the function." You "castrate and bid the geldings be fruitful."[13] This comes home with a vengeance in your conclusion, where you talk about what you want the human race to do. "One of the greatest challenges facing civilization in the twenty-first century is for human beings to learn to speak about their deepest personal concerns—about ethics, spiritual experience, and the inevitability of human suffering—in ways that are not flagrantly irrational" (87). You write here as though our "deepest personal concerns" have value. As we make "ethical" choices, as we experience something "spiritual," and as we contemplate the horror of human "suffering," you write and say that we have to learn how to speak about these things. I put scare quotes around those three words because on your account I am one set of complex chemical reactions secreting something that I falsely believe to be arguments to another set of complex chemical reactions who falsely believes that he is reading them.

"We must find ways to invoke the power of ritual and to mark those transitions in every human life that demand profundity—birth, marriage, death—without lying to ourselves about the nature of reality" (88). You want life to have meaning, and you want it to have meaning without shrinking back from the intellectual demands of raw atheism. In short, you want to square

13. C.S. Lewis, *The Abolition of Man* (New York: Macmillan, 1955), 35.

the circle, and you cannot do it. But you keep trying. "But any genuine exploration of ethics or the contemplative life demand the same standards of reasonableness and self-criticism that animate all intellectual discourse" (90). But if you apply reason and self-criticism to an atheistic examination of ethics, you should discover within ten minutes *that there aren't any.*

You say we must speak about these things, and you demand at the front end intellectual honesty. "We desperately need a public discourse that encourages critical thinking and intellectual honesty" (87). Well, here is the honest answer: You are a hodge-podge of neuron-firings looking into an abyss which you only *think* you understand. You don't really understand it because you are not thinking at all, but rather doing what chemicals always do under those conditions and at that temperature. Consequently, you have no reason to believe that anything you think is true, *including* the idea that all your thoughts are chemical reactions. You present yourself as willing to embrace the stark realities, but when you talk about ethics, *spiritual* experience, and concern over suffering, you give the game away. That is not atheism, but rather residue from your culture's Christian past.

You still want to speak as though the arrival of Darwin and secular enlightenment set us all free from some really bad stuff. "The truth is, some of your most cherished beliefs are as embarrassing as those that sent the last slave ship sailing to America as late as 1859 (the same year that Darwin published *The Origin of Species*)" (88). Your implication is clear. Before Darwin, slavery. After Darwin, sweetness and light. But you really need to take a close look at the racist implications of Darwinism, and how those implications were *understood* and applied in the eugenics movement leading up to the Holocaust. The recent book *From Darwin to Hitler* spells it out pretty plainly.[14] Of course, I expect you to protest that such linkage is a historical slander, and that I am misrepresenting Darwinism's link to racism. But the facts speak for themselves, and you have been insisting that we follow the argument wherever it leads. So here is the argument. Given the fact that human beings evolved from primates, as you asserted earlier, is there any *a priori* reason why a *consistent* evolutionist wouldn't cheerfully agree that one race of human beings could certainly be lower on the evolutionary tree than the others? Any reason why, when we get to *homo sapiens*, magic suddenly intervenes and equality appears? YOU might believe in this equality (for social reasons), but Darwin and the entirety of his early entourage certainly didn't. Those of us who believe that all human races are descended from Noah don't struggle with the same problem, because we are all *human* cousins.

---

14. Richard Weikart, *From Darwin to Hitler* (New York: Palgrave Macmillan, 2004).

While lamenting the violence that religion has brought into the world, your language toward believers sometimes verges on the violent. "Only then will the practice of raising our children to believe that they are Christian, Muslim, or Jewish be widely recognized as the ludicrous obscenity that it is" (88). "Ludicrous obscenity?" Isn't exposing minors to obscenity a form of child abuse? Do you think children should be forcibly removed from such homes? You allow that religion may have bestowed some sort of evolutionary advantage at some point in our history, but you do not throw this out as a compliment. You think the same thing about rape. "There is, after all, nothing more natural than rape. But no one would argue that rape is good, or compatible with a civil society, because it may have had evolutionary advantages for our ancestors" (91). As with rape, so with religion. May have been useful once, but not anymore.

You lament "the failure of our schools to announce the death of God in a way that each generation can understand" (91). That failure is a necessary one. Mankind was created by God, and despite man's sin, we cannot shake the reality of that createdness from ourselves. Public schools certainly can't do it. Nothing can alter the fundamental way in which God has configured the world. Arguments with gravity are difficult to maintain.

And this leads to the second part of this last installment. Bits and pieces of what I am about to say have been sprinkled throughout this short book, but I wanted to make sure that at some point I stated the whole thing together in some sort of coherent fashion. I said earlier that mankind is all screwed up. But this is not because we crawled out of the primordial ooze, not yet arriving at our evolutionary destination. In the gospel, the Christian Church declares that man has fallen from his first estate. In other words, we believe in *devolution*, not evolution.

God created us morally upright, able to have fellowship with Him, and we rejected this—rebelling for the sake of autonomy. A desire to maintain that same autonomy is manifest throughout your book. You want to think the way you want to think. When Adam and Eve were being tempted in the Garden, they saw that the fruit was good for food, pleasant to the eyes, and suitable to make them wise. This threefold temptation corresponded to something the apostle John wrote many centuries later—Christians are charged to avoid worldliness, and this means avoiding "the lust of the flesh, and the lust of the eyes, and the pride of life" (1 John 2:16). The lust of the flesh corresponds to the fruit as food, the lust of the eyes corresponds to its pleasing appearance, and the pride of life (the real center of all the mischief) corresponds to the autonomous desire to be like God.

When Adam rebelled against God, the entire human race was plunged into sin. We were not only hurled headlong into a great ocean of sins and sinning, but into the very condition of sin itself. Every aspect of our being was polluted in this fall. We do not just *do* bad things; we do them because we *are* bad people. Your book pointed out many of the bad things we do. You attributed this to "religion," but it would be much closer to the mark to attribute it to "people." You are quite right about one thing though. Religion doesn't fix the problem, and in many cases, it just compounds the problem. Two inches of snow on a dung heap can look pretty nice, but it doesn't address the deeper problem. So if we sinful men go left, we sin on the left. If we go right, we sin on the right. If we become atheists, we sin there. If we become Jehovah's Witnesses, we sin there. *Wherever we go, there we are.* The generic category of "religion" cannot help us in this anymore than the abstract concept of "medicine" can help us when we are sick. We need *actual* medicine, not the *idea* of medicine. And this is why we need Christ, not mere religion.

And so, according to the gospel, the entire human race was captured in this state of death. We live out our pathetic lives in this death. But just as the head of our race, Adam, got us into this slavery of sin, so God resolved to provide salvation by the same means. An Adam got us into this, and an Adam was God's choice to get us out. This is why Jesus Christ was born into our race—so He could become the last Adam and the founder of a new humanity. This is what the Christian Church actually *is*—humanity reconstituted in Christ. This may seem to you to be nothing more than an arrogant hypersectarianism, but it really is not. This is because the prophets proclaimed that in Christ the entire world would be efficaciously forgiven, delivered, and restored in their humanity. This is not a message for a mystery cult tucked away in a corner somewhere; it is good news for the entire world.

Because of our sinfulness and sins, we all deserved the sentence of death and hell forever. But instead of this, Christ came to offer a glorious exchange. All our sins would be placed on Him, and all His righteousness would be placed on us (2 Cor. 5:21). In its culmination, this transaction occurred at the cross. Jesus died, and in that death He embraced the pollutions of a very polluted world. He took onto Himself the wrath and anger of God, and He did this so that in Him we might become the righteousness of God. He gathered up a world full of hatred, adultery, treachery, rape, murder, envy, genocide, religious hypocrisy, atheism, theft, lying, and all forms of arrogant haughtiness, gathered it all to His chest, and disappearing, sank into death.

But what looked like death and sin overwhelming the Messiah was actually the Messiah overwhelming death and sin. That uncanny, numinous moment was actually the death of death in the death of Christ. God determined that our Lord's wonderful sacrifice would be the hinge upon which the new world would turn. Because Jesus rose from the dead, leaving the sin behind Him in the grave, we who have been joined with Him in that death are also joined with Him in His resurrection. And this is what we mean when we refer to what it means to be born again; we are regenerated in order that we might walk with Him in newness of life. All the blessings that God is willing to give to humanity are right *there*, in the death, burial and resurrection of Jesus Christ. This is the gospel.

The apostle Paul teaches us in the first chapter of Romans (1:21) that there are two particular aspects of the creature's relationship to God that sinful men want to suppress or deny. The first is the sovereignty of God, or, if you like, the *Godness* of God. We have already covered this earlier in our discussion of the Asian tsunami and Hurricane Katrina. God disposes of His creation as He pleases. But even when it comes to expressions of God's severity, the apostle talks about it in a context that sees rebellious men coming back to Him in repentance (Rom. 11:22–23). The fundamental orientation of God to our sinful world is one of redemptive love, not annihilating wrath (John 3:17). The wrath is a reality, but the basic expression of it is seen in the cross, where Jesus suffered the wrath of God for the sins of His people. Wrath and love met in the cross, and this is why we as sinners can be saved.

Because of the death of Jesus, the world is *delivered* from the wrath of God (1 John 2:1–2).

And this leads to the second thing that sinful men want to get away from, which is the obligation to be thankful (Rom. 1:21). One of the principal failings in atheism is that it leaves us with no one to thank for the countless blessings we encounter daily. This extends from trivial things, like the pleasure we get from pulling our socks up, to more amazing gifts, like food and music and marriage. And of course, the capstone of all our gratitude is thanksgiving for what the New Testament describes as the "indescribable gift" (2 Cor. 9:15)—the gospel of our Lord Jesus. Jesus died and rose to straighten it all out, and that is what He is doing.

Now I know that if you have read this far, it is probably because you are just "indulging the preacher." But I do want you to know that I know that this sounds like gibberish to you. As an argument, I know that it seems beyond strange. "A Jewish carpenter was executed by the authorities of Jerusalem two thousand years ago, and this happened so that our sins could be forgiven?" So why do I repeat it then, *knowing* how strange it sounds to you? Well, the answer is that God has promised to transform the entire world—a multitude beyond all counting was promised to Abraham—as people listen to this particular story being told. And for two thousand years He has been doing exactly that. And Christians will continue to tell it until He stops fulfilling His Word, which means that this is *the* story that will be told to the end of the world.

May the Lord call you to Himself on the basis of this kind gospel. But whether He does this or not, if we ever meet, I would love to buy you a beer.

FOR FURTHER READING

G.K. Chesteron, *Orthodoxy* (New York: Image Books, 1908).

C.S. Lewis, *Mere Christianity* (New York: Macmillan, 1943).

Greg Bahnsen, *Always Ready* (Atlanta, GA: American Vision, 1996).

Gary DeMar, *Pushing the Antithesis* (Atlanta, GA: American Vision, 2007).

Douglas Wilson, *Clean Water, Red Wine, Broken Bread* (Moscow, ID: Canon Press, 2000).

John Frame, *Apologetics to the Glory of God* (Phillipsburg, NJ: Presbyterian and Reformed, 1994).

GOD IS

HOW CHRISTIANITY
EXPLAINS EVERYTHING

PREFACE

I t may appear to the casual observer that a few years ago someone gave a signal and a new wave of militant atheists began publishing books like crazy. These books contain many or most of the standard arguments against God, but *something* is different. The zeal, the militancy, and the underlying sense of panic indicate some kind of sea change in the relationship between believers and unbelievers.

I believe it is necessary to answer the challenges, but it is also necessary to resist the temptation to be shrill in response. The issues are important, but no sense getting really worked up over it. If we were all sitting on a used car lot, and one of the F-250 trucks began questioning the existence of Henry Ford, we would all think it was a serious situation, but that is not the same thing as thinking it a serious question.

I have answered Sam Harris in a short little book called *Letter from a Christian Citizen*. This is my second book that seeks to address and answer the new wave of atheist challenges, and it is a response to *God is Not Great* by Christopher Hitchens. Those who have read the first book will recognize that some of the structural arguments in this one follow the same pattern, but it is still important to give each author his due, and to follow the ins and outs of the entire discussion. It would be foolish to think that a study of the battle of Gettysburg was the same as studying the battle of Waterloo because "they both had guns."

If this subject interests you, as it does many, it is my hope that you will enjoy the discussion, and, when you are done, that you will say a prayer for Christopher Hitchens's soul.[1]

---

1. This paragraph was written when Christopher Hitchens was still alive. And while what is done is done, I would still urge everyone to pray for those that Hitch influenced. And I can mention that I do know that he had at least one opportunity to consider the gospel after he was diagnosed with the cancer that killed him.

CHAPTER 1

LO, THE BOMBASTICATOR COMETH

C o mes now Christopher Hitchens in his new book, *God Is Not Great,* and he thwacketh us believers upon the mazzard.

The book promises to be an engaging read; Hitchens writes fluidly and well, and he knows how to go over the top rhetorically, but not by too much. There will be more on this shortly. His rationalism is very much in evidence, but he does not write like so many other atheistic rationalists—men who believe that the authority of reason (all rise!) necessitates a turgid kind of book that acts like it was put together by a committee of certified public accountants trying to write a phone directory. As though *that* were a rational thing to do.

But Hitchens promises better than this. His prose is hale and hardy; he recognizes and appreciates good writing elsewhere, and he uses it consistently himself. And it is a good thing too, because it appears that this is all he has.

I need to change the subject for just a moment, but I am not really doing so. I do have a point here. Suppose you went to see some fantastic illusionist, and he did something remarkable, like levitate himself. His beautiful assistant with insufficient clothing—and this might have something to do with the success of the trick, actually—comes out on stage and passes some metal hoops every which way around the floating body. Jeepers, you think, and head on home scratching your noggin. When you get there, you find yourself in a discussion with your cousin who used to do a smalltime illusionist act of his own down at the local Ramada Inn, and he explains to you how the trick is done. He doesn't have to be a big-time headliner; he just has to have enough experience to be able to explain how such tricks are pulled off.

I am the Ramada Inn guy, only drop the illusionist aspect now. I write a lot, like Hitchens does, and I know how to put a sentence or two together. I believe I also know how to make a metaphor crawl up your back and make an unpleasant smacky noise in your ear. Or, more pleasantly, to get a couple of cute zephyrs to fool around with your hair on a warm spring day. Here, pick a card, any card.

To get right to the point, I can tell *exactly* what Hitchens is doing, and how he is doing it. As we work through his book together, I am going to point it out for you. But do not think that I will do anything so trite and rationalistic as objecting to his use of rhetoric or wordsmithing showmanship. "That's just rhetoric" is a simplistic objection. Rhetoric is not to be thought of as the M&Ms or chocolate sprinkles that you use to decorate the top of your frozen yogurt. It is not a mere flourish to adorn an otherwise *bleh* argument. Rhetorical abilities are an essential part of argument itself, and this is why, when someone like Hitchens (obviously gifted in this) turns those abilities against God, he is revealing far more than he knows. Or perhaps not . . . Hitchens begins by trying to take away that possible response. Those who point out the "sins and deformities that animated" Hitchens to write this book are revealing that *they* are the ones with the problem (1).[2]

As just mentioned, Hitchens is unlike other atheist writers in his ability to write. But in one sad fact, he is just like them. He is morally indignant. Instead of taking refuge in the (relatively) strong fortress of nihilistic relativism and laughing at all the poor blinkered dopes who think that truth and beauty are still

---

2. Throughout this book, the page numbers given in parentheses refer to Christopher Hitchens, *God Is Not Great: How Religion Poisons Everything* (New York: Twelve, 2007).

ambulatory in this sorry world, Hitchens (like *all* these other recently published guys) calls us and raises us ten. "You have puritanical indignation at our unbelief? Well, watch *this*." And the atheist, a complex chemical reaction, according to the best contemporary science, uncorks with scathing observations on the hypocrisies of other complex chemical reactions. Hitchens does this in the first five lines of his book, and he shows no sign of letting up. But how can a chemical reaction be hypocritical? How can the chemical reaction that is man be a hypocrite? Given his premises, it is like being indignant with a tornado, or some random rutabaga, or sand on the beach—but Hitchens does it. They all do it. This is a point that I have made before in my interactions with Sam Harris, and with Richard Dawkins, and with various others before them. I am happy to make the point again, and it should not distress any of us that I am doing so. An argument is like a tool; you put it down when the job is done, and not when you are tired of holding it. When atheists stop suspending their moral indignation from their invisible sky hook, then I will no longer amuse myself by pointing out *their* levitation trick. I can answer Hitchens on this point with an argument condensed into one word. Not only that, but I will condense it into a word with only two characters in it. Three if you count the question mark: *so?*

Religion poisons everything. So?

The fact that the argument can admit of such elegant economy does not mean that it cannot be expanded, like this. Religion poisons everything. "So? Does this offend anyone whose opinion should matter to me? Is there some kind of rule against poisoning everything? Who made *that* rule? And who died and left that particular busybody king? Get your moralism outa my *face*, Hitchens." Now this response should not be confounded with anything so juvenile as a Bronx cheer. This is an *argument*, not a raspberry.

When Hitchens says that religion poisons everything, he says this as though it were a bad thing. He doesn't *show* that it is a bad thing. He doesn't prove that it is a bad thing. He doesn't demonstrate that it is a bad thing. He just rummages around in all the old Sunday School lessons from his upbringing, hidden in some shoebox in his intellectual attic, blows the dust off his best sanctimonious judgmentalism, and declares that we all must submit to the Word from his attic. "Thou shalt not poison everything." Sez *who*?

Lots of people think lots of things are bad, and not all of them are, and who are *they* to tell me what to do anyway? Some are right, some are wrong, and others are simply incoherent. Let's start with those who are simply wrong. They tell me that Allah is the one true God, and Mohammad is his prophet, and I have to drop everything and do just what they say. I am a

Christian, so I believe this is an error, but at least it is coherent. If Allah *were* God, we *should* do what He says. An incoherent approach would go something like this: "There is no God; there is no fixed standard of morality overarching all of us, and so we must all pull together and submit to the resultant fixed standard." I don't get it either.

If Hitchens is merely saying that Christians frequently don't meet the standards of their own Christian faith, he is doing nothing remarkable. If he is pointing out such internal inconsistencies, then he is welcome to add his voice to the long and honored line of prophetic denunciation. There is nothing in that approach that the prophet Amos wouldn't be good with. But this is not what he is doing. He is assuming that Christians are offending against a standard that overarches believers and nonbelievers alike, and that this standard is clearly obligatory on everybody.

Now pretend I am a simpleton. Hitchens went up these stairs three at a time, and I must have missed something. Explain it to me *slowly*. "God does not exist. Therefore all people have a fixed moral obligation to not poison everything *because* . . ." What goes after that because? Because the universe doesn't give a rip? Because in two hundred years, we will all be dead? Because moral conventions are just that, social *conventions*? Give me something to follow that *because* that is derived from the premises of atheism and that clearly and compellingly requires nonatheists to submit to it as well. Is that too much to ask? Apparently.

The assumed standard (inevitably) has to be the result of mixing reason and science together in some magical way. He doesn't argue for it, but he does assume it. Hitchens wants unbelief to be in a class by itself. No rented square footage in the marketplace of ideas for him.

> Our belief is not a belief. Our principles are not a faith. We do not rely solely upon science and reason, because these are necessary rather than sufficient factors, but we distrust anything that contradicts science or outrages reason. We may differ on many things, but what we respect is free inquiry, openmindedness, and the pursuit of ideas for their own sake. (5)

In this notable expression of high sentiment, Hitchens declares that he distrusts anything that outrages reason. And just before this, he delivered himself of the zen-mystery that "our belief is not a belief." Okay, so he has faith in certain of his principles, but this faith of his is not like our faith in our principles because ours are . . . wrong. His faith in his principles is not faith at all. It is something else. It is confidence, yeah, that's it, confidence. *Con fides*. With faith. And his beliefs are not like our beliefs, not at all. No, his beliefs, which are not beliefs, are based on certain beliefs about science and reason.

David Hume had a mighty hard time figuring out how to get across the chasm from *is* to *ought*. Mr. Hitchens must have figured out how to do this, because he has gotten from the *is* of repeatable experiments, and the *is* of the law of identity, to the *ought* of "Thou shalt not poison everything." This is a stupendous breakthrough. And Mr. Hitchens needs to do this whole math problem on the board, in front of the class, and Mr. Hitchens needs to *show his work*.

Hitchens points out that some believers respond badly to his kind of bad boy atheism, and this is something I grant. In fact, I am perfectly willing to loan him a fixed scriptural standard so that he might enjoy the pleasure of disapproving of hysterical believers who go off like a bottle rocket whenever an atheist is naughty in public. But that is the only way he is able to enjoy such spectacles—*with borrowed standards*. When believers panic or hyperventilate over the monkeyshines of men like Hitchens, they *are* displeasing Jesus. But are they displeasing the mindless process of time and chance acting on matter, which is all that anything or anyone actually is? Well, it turns out, no.

In Hitchens's view, according to his premises, Christian hypocrisies (a source of amusement to many for millennia) turn out to be just another big dud in a universe of big duds. The infinite concourse of atoms supplies us with nothing more than an endless supply of dropped punch lines. But the Puritan Nathaniel

Ward had more to feed on than this; he said he had only two consolations in this life—the perfections of Christ and the imperfections of Christians.

But not *all* Christians are threatened in the way Hitchens describes. There are believers who are secure in their faith and who respond to atheistic blowfish faces on our windows with the appropriate amusement. We *are* out here. There are *many* of us. And if you want to know who we are, we are gentlemen of Jap . . . no, wait, wrong groove.

CHAPTER 2

WET STREETS CAUSE RAIN

The second chapter of Hitchens's book is entitled "Religion Kills." Well, in this world of hardscrabble Darwinism, nature red in tooth and claw, what doesn't? Religion kills, but so does cancer, old age, hunting accidents, radiation from the sun, other predatory species, too much mayonnaise, and the music of Andrew Lloyd Webber. Actually, we need to take the wide-angle lens and admit that it is evolution that kills.

There are two things that can be said in response to this second chapter of Hitchens's book. The first is what was said in the last chapter—*Killing is bad? Who says that? Is there a reason we must listen to him? Is it bad to not listen to him?* But let us not become tiresome. We will return to flog this dead horse only when it tries to get up again, which is probably just a few pages away.

But the second response is to point out the logical problem with how Hitchens has arranged his thought experiment. Suppose his thesis was not that religion poisons everything, but rather that trousers poison everything. Since trousers are common enough, just like religion, it would not be much work at all for a person of Hitchens's abilities to assemble one horrendous story after another of one atrocity after another, and all committed by men in *trousers*. See? Trousers poison everything.

The problem here is immediately seen in the availability of counterexamples. We betake ourselves to look at *this* society, and then *that* one, and all the men in those societies wear togas. And, sure enough, we find that all the same atrocities are being committed in these differently appareled cultures. Maybe trousers don't poison everything. Maybe men are a disgrace to trousers. For if trousers poisoned everything, one would think (naturally enough) that to get into a trouser-free zone would pretty much take care of the problem. But toga men do all the same kind of awful stuff. And then, so do loincloth men. Maybe togas don't poison everything either. Maybe men are a disgrace to togas.

The subtitle of this book is *How Religion Poisons Everything*. And in this chapter, "Religion Kills,"

Hitchens points to example after example of religious people behaving badly. And I, for one, don't think he is making this stuff up. But for someone who bases an awful lot on *reason*, I think he needs to pay closer attention to what he is doing in the name thereof. His conclusion does not follow from the evidence being presented, not unless wet streets cause rain.

Perhaps Hitchens should take a step farther back and argue a much more plausible point, which is that "People Poison Everything." Go back to our trouser example. If trousers were the problem, then getting rid of them should get rid of the basic problem (making all due allowance for societal inertia). In the same way, if religion is the toxic waste in the system, then purging it should deal with the problem. So, then, what have almost a century of religion-free societies (Soviet Union, Red China, and so on) taught us about all this? We ought to have had quite a few trips around the sun enjoying life to its fullest, now that religion (that which poisons everything) was banished and gone. But, son of a gun, the atrocities sort of picked up a considerable amount of speed. The "poison" was purged from the system, but the patient was still flat on his back on the hospital bed with his tongue hanging out.

When you look at abominable theistic societies and abominable atheistic societies, the variables are probably not the thing you want to appeal to in order to account for the constant, horrific result. We need to look for the constant. What might that be? *People.* People poison everything. The Scriptures give us the reason for this, which is that people are sinners.

There are two reasons why someone like Hitchens cannot make this obvious connection. The first is that he is a humanist. He appeals to the "elementary duty of a self-respecting human" (28). To admit that people are corrupt in themselves, rather than corrupted from the outside by a very convenient bogey like religion, would be to admit a fundamental corruption in what is Hitchens's functional deity. Man is basically *good.* Bad things come from *other* places, and *other* sources. This approach enables Hitchens to be as cynical as he wants about what is going on out there, while at the same time not blaspheming what he believes to be man's essential goodness at the core.

And, second, to admit that man is a sinner—clumps of sin all over his clod-hopping, mud-encrusted boots—is to admit that *he* is the one bringing the problems into everything else. But this is sounding too much like orthodox Christianity, and this is nothing other than an affirmation of a basic Christian truth. Man is a sinner, and he brings sin into everything—into politics, into religion, into philanthropy, into car sales, into professional sports, into windsurfing, into war, into painting, into Little League baseball. This is the trouble. People poison everything. Wherever we go, there we are.

CHAPTER 3

FOOLISHNESS TO THE GREEKS

C hapter Three is "A Short Digression on the Pig; or, Why Heaven Hates Ham." Since it is a brief chapter, it warrants a response of comparable length. In it, Hitchens has a case of the cutes—there is a lot here to make fun of, which is something he is good at, so he veers away from his unfolding argument to let us know why Heaven hates ham. "All religions have a tendency to feature some dietary injunction or prohibition" (37).

In addition to this religious preoccupation with avoiding some foods, Hitchens points out that the pig comes in for special treatment. Not only do Jews avoid it, but so (ironically) do the Muslims. "Real horror of the porcine is manifest all over the Islamic world" (38). There are three problems with this brief chapter.

The first is the architectural problem with his argument, and it is the same one we encountered in the previous post. He is right that food restrictions are a very common feature of world religions. The one notable exception is the Christian faith—Christ declared all foods clean, and this declaration is a notable type of the gospel being offered to all nations, as St. Peter discovered. But even though this is the case, it is still true that the perennial human desire to restrict certain foods has crept back into Christianity in various ways and guises. Hitchens cites the now-relaxed Catholic deal of fish on Fridays, but plenty of Protestants have gone in for various food fads as an aid to combating the sinful desires within—corn flakes and graham crackers, at their inception, being just a few examples of purported edible aids to sexual purity.

But here is the structural problem with Hitchens's argument. Is this something that *religion* does (uniquely), or is it something that *people* do? A universal tendency toward a certain practice will usually take on religious trappings in religious societies, but a brief look around us today should reveal that secularists who have lost their faith in God have certainly *not* lost their faith in the ability of foodstuffs to align them to the world properly. Allow me to invite your average secularist devotee of the Food Co-op over for lunch. I will fix him a sandwich—Skippy peanut butter out of a jar purchased at Safeway, a couple slices of Wonder Bread—the puffy white kind, and brown sugar. I bet I can get them to look at it the way a Hasidic rabbi would eye a BLT. And it would be a perfectly good lunch too.

A second problem is that Hitchens reveals here (not that we didn't already know) that he believes in evolution. Speaking of the pig, he says, "I hope that you have guessed by now what we know in any case— that this fine beast is one of our fairly close cousins. It shares a great deal of our DNA . . ." (38–39). It should just be noted here that the obvious commonality is being taken as evidence for common ancestry, when it could just as easily be taken for the desire of a common Creator to use certain ideas over again. To argue that the Ford Taurus evolved from the Model T because they each have four tires is a dubious procedure. Maybe four tires is just a good idea, and anybody who wants to build a car should use it. Maybe a pig liver does the same thing that a human liver does, and for similar reasons. A Chevy and a Ford both have tailpipes, and I am entirely in favor of this. There is no doubt a common reason for it, and we need not resort to the explanation that the two cars are cousins, sharing a common ancestor.

And last, Hitchens is to be faulted because, without knowing it, he almost stumbled into the gospel. He explains our fascination with the pig as an example of simultaneous attraction and revulsion.

> The simultaneous attraction and repulsion derived from an anthropomorphic root: the look of the pig, and the taste of the pig, and the dying yells of the pig, and the evident intelligence of the pig, were too uncomfortably reminiscent of the human. (40)

Hitchens relies (in part) on Sir James Frazer and his out-of-date anthropology. The out-of-dateness is reflected in Hitchens's treatment of this business, having that breathless debunking spirit that Victorian infidels exhibited when they tried to rattle Christians by pointing out that pagan temples had spires, too, just like churches. In this instance, Hitchens expects us to be astonished beyond measure when we discover that human sacrifice was the foundation for ancient animal sacrifices. *But of course it was.* The entire gospel is based on human sacrifice. Apart from the shedding of blood there is no remission of sin (Heb. 9:22), and the blood that needed to be shed was *human* blood. Animal sacrifices were always a pale substitute for this, and the gospel of Jesus Christ is the declaration of God that all foundational murders have had the self-justifying cover ripped off of them for good.

I would recommend in the future that Hitchens rely on anthropology that is not a century or more in the rearview mirror—not because his point here is an invalid one, but rather because it is a point that does not go nearly far enough. He apparently believes that Christians will recoil, aghast, when he informs us that animal sacrifice was a stand-in for human sacrifice. Of course it was; that was the whole *point*.

Moreover, throughout the Old Testament, this story is always told without flinching, and in the New Testament, the death of Christ is told from the standpoint of the victim of the judicial murder. Hitchens needs to read a little of the work of René Girard. This is the story that will be told till the end of the world, and it is the story that annihilates human sacrifice. Contrast this with the peaceful, mythic stories of the ancient infidels, who could always be counted on to draw a thick veil over their foundational murders, calling it their serenity and peace.

The Bible is a bloody book, all right, but it is blood that *deals* with our sins—as opposed to the blood that must be covered up with various edifying and inspiring stories. This is the gospel—with death and resurrection front and center. If Hitchens wants us to be embarrassed about this, this too is a fulfillment of Scripture. This message is foolishness to the Greeks, among whom we may certainly number Mr. Hitchens.

CHAPTER 4

WOULD THERE BE A VICE SQUAD IN HITCHENSVILLE?

The next chapter is Hitchens on health, to which the religion of your choice is almost certainly hazardous.

We are only on the fourth chapter, and it is of average length, but the mistakes Hitchens makes are starting to accumulate, so it might take a little bit of extra time to get a front loader in here and clean this up.

The first problem is one mentioned already. For Hitchens to point out all the problems in the world and blame them on "religion" is like writing a book attacking "medicine," that well-meaning endeavor which has killed its untold millions. But to get this result we must define medicine as "anything that comes promising relief in bottles or any other container." That kind of categorization positively *promises* to blur vital distinctions, like the difference we might want to acknowledge that exists between penicillin and Cousin Bob's Juju Beans Cancer Therapy, three bucks a bottle. But Hitchens is on the offensive here. "Why make such distinctions? Why confound the issues? Whence this bigoted defense of 'medicine?' Are you *denying* that the chicken bones thrown in the air is sheer charlatanism?" Well, no . . .

The second issue, ironically, is Hitchens castigating religions for being obscurantist when it comes to simple, easy, and readily available cures for eradicable diseases such as polio. He cites the example of some Muslim imams issuing a fatwa against the simple ingesting of some drops that would eradicate that disease completely. He emphasizes the needless suffering that "religion" has inflicted here. I take his point, although, again, I am in the position of the penicillin advocate who finds himself called upon to defend the chicken bone treatment because both were administered during "doctor visits," and Hitchens has written quite a strident book against "doctor visits."

I am still glad he picked this argument. Since religion poisons everything, let's talk about DDT and malaria. Let's talk about which religious group it was that succeeded in banning a substance that would have saved hundreds of thousands of lives. Was it the Vatican, or

Muslim imams, or . . . sorry? Oh, it was *secularists* who in one of their periodic and recurring enviropanics decided to consign countless thousands in the Third World to misery and death? But this wasn't a *religious* bonehead move? Can we still count it, or does it have to go into another book?

Further, one of his examples of this religious obscurantism was the claim by some Roman Catholic officials who were out there saying that condoms were not really the hot stuff in preventing AIDS. *Oh, tempora! Oh, mores!*

> Would you care to see my video of the advice given by Cardinal Alfonso Lopez de Trujillo, the Vatican's president of the Pontifical Council for the Family, carefully warning his audience that all condoms are secretly made with many microscopic holes, through which the AIDS virus can pass? (45)

Well, let us keep this one simple, and not get into the extraneous issues. What *size* is the HIV virus, since we have all been exhorted to ask *scientific* questions? And what is the actual size (again, scientifically speaking) of the mesh that a condom provides?

Condoms are designed to prevent the passage of the spermatazoon, and the HIV virus is *450 times smaller* than the spermatazoon. And exactly how is this not like trying to keep mosquitoes out of your yard with a chain link fence? But even if the particular answer is wrong, is this not a *reasonable* question? But Hitchens just waves the word *science* in our faces, expecting us to just shut up about it. If a cardinal raises the issue (which, it would seem, is a reasonable issue for science and reason to raise), Hitchens simply dismisses him as a "wicked" lunatic.

The third issue is sex itself. We were bound to get here sooner or later. It appears that religious folks are as uptight as it gets, and we all need to unzip a little—so we can *really* get the aforementioned AIDS crisis going and give the scientists something to work on that is really worthy of their majestic powers. Actually, Hitchens doesn't say anything like that, but he does say something every bit as silly. "The New Testament has Saint Paul expressing both fear and contempt for the female" (54). It would have been nice for Hitchens to put a few references in there (3 Corinthians 9:13, Hezekiah 3:16) so that we could at least know *which* verses he was misunderstanding. But, alas, he did not have time.

Hitchens does cite some Muslim travesties as evidence for his position, but even here, with such an inviting target, he misses it wide. Islam *does* have a problem with women enjoying sex, and the browbeating of women that goes on in the name of Allah does seem to me to indicate a deep-seated masculinist insecurity over sexual performance. But the way Hitchens refers to this is just risible.

"I simply laugh when I read the Koran, with its endless prohibitions on sex and its corrupt promise of infinite debauchery in the life to come" (55). Yeah, right. This, written about a religion which allows each Muslim male to have up to four wives and as many slave girls as the proud owner of them can mount. This, written about a religion that awards faithful men at least three score and ten virgins in the paradise hereafter, not to mention sexual access to all the cute little Ganymede boys. Islam *is* all screwed up when it comes to sex, but the problem is not that the men aren't getting any. Hardly. The problem is that their worship of raw power has turned their conception of everything sexual into some form of rape. And here is where Hitchens veers off into breathtaking naïveté.

"The homicidal lunatics . . . of 9/11 were perhaps tempted by virgins, but it is far more revolting to contemplate that, like so many of their fellow jihadists, they were virgins" (55). Anybody who believes that these guys were virgins needs to be given a time out from public policy discourse for at least three weeks. We could give him some books to read during those three weeks, but we don't really need to—there is material enough to refute Hitchens on this point from this very chapter.

And last, Hitchens has, on at least three occasions in this chapter, inveighed against a particular practice as engaged in by religious types, and then, within a page or so, he does the very same thing himself. Example numero uno:

> Those who preached hatred and fear and guilt and who ruined innumerable childhoods should have been thankful that the hell they preached was only one among their wicked falsifications, and that they were not sent to rot there. (56)

And, then, next page, before he has had time even to catch his breath:

> Tertullian . . . was perhaps clever in going for the lowest common denominator and promising that one of the most intense pleasures of the afterlife would be endless contemplation of the tortures of the damned. (57)

It appears from these two quotations taken together that Hitchens thinks that one of the only possible arguments against atheism is that he won't be allowed to watch people like Tertullian burn.

A second example of this is when Hitchens faults Tim LaHaye and Jerry B. Jenkins, not so much for prose bad enough to make the back teeth ache, but rather for (presumably gleefully) looking forward to the bloodbath of Armageddon. *Bad* evangelicals. Julia Ward Howe gets the same treatment.

> One of the very many connections between religious belief and the sinister, spoiled, selfish childhood of our species is the repressed desire to see everything smashed up and ruined and brought to naught. (57)

But what do we discover on the very next page? We have some billions of years to go yet, but even Hitchens cannot abstain from the glee that apparently afflicts all our species.

> At around that point, it will emulate millions of other suns and explosively mutate into a swollen 'red giant,' causing the earth's oceans to boil and extinguishing all possibility of life in any form. No description by any prophet or visionary has even begun to picture the awful intensity and irrevocability of that moment. (58)

The good news is that since this whole thing is a repression issue, Hitchens is probably not even aware of the jollies he got out of that paragraph.

Last example: "Can it be a coincidence, then, that all religions claim the right to legislate in matters of sex?" (53). For those following one of my central objections to Hitchens, it would be closer to the mark to say that all human societies, *religious or not*, claim the right to legislate in matters of sex. This includes Hitchensville. "But the conscription of the unprotected child for these purposes is something that even the most dedicated secularist can safely describe as sin" (52). Yeah, you can *describe* it as sin all right. You just can't defend your position when asked about it. *Why* is it a sin?

In this section, Hitchens is talking about an abuse of children that goes beyond sexual abuse, but let us

limit our discussion to sexual abuse, just to keep ourselves focused on the central issue. Hitchens is not
shy about telling us how he *feels* about this. "This revulsion is innate in any healthy person, and does not
need to be taught" (52). What we don't know is why
Hitchens-sentiment is the arbiter of what constitutes
"any healthy person," and why, since it does not need
even to be taught, some people in San Francisco and
the Boston diocese seemed never to have learned it.
Imagine there's no Hell below us, it's easy if you try,
and this is true even if a man has ruined the child-
hoods of a thousand kids.

Why is Hitchens-sentiment authoritative over the
yearnings (quite powerful) of the president of the
North American Man-Boy Love Association? And what
does Hitchens-sentiment do when said president gives
him the raspberry and heads off for another night of
carnal relations? And what would Hitchens say if the
man stopped giving him the raspberry, in order to ask
a simple question: "*Why* is my desire for boys wrong?
No god prohibited it, according to you, and *your* feelings are not my god, according to me."

The strength of Hitchens's feelings about this would
seem to indicate that the answer to such a question
would be an easy one. So what is it?

CHAPTER 5

BECAUSE MY BRAIN BURBLES

I t used to be possible for believers to have a brain, but no more. This is because our ancestors lived in the blackest of ignorance, and theologians like Aquinas or Maimonides were just playing cards with the hand they were dealt. Ya know?

I said in an earlier chapter that I was going to point out some of Hitchens's rhetorical funny business when he substituted it for argument. He does that here like an expert, fluffing himself up like one of those puffer birds, and the song is almost like a chortle.

Back in the day, *nobody* "had the smallest idea what idea what was going on" (64). You know, like we do today. *Now* we know lots and lots about the "natural order," like gravity 'n' stuff.

> Today the least educated of my children knows much more about the natural order than any of the founders of religion All attempts to reconcile faith with science and reason are consigned to failure and ridicule for precisely these reasons. (64–65)

But Hitchens doffs his hat to the medieval *ignorati* anyway.

> The scholastic obsessives of the Middle Ages were doing the best they could on the basis of hopelessly limited information, ever-present fear of death and judgment, very low life expectancy, and an audience of illiterates. (68)

In distinction to the audience that Hitchens is privileged to have, all proud graduates of our government school system. You know, illiteracy and functional illiteracy have not gone away—what has gone away is the money we spend fighting illiteracy. After the publication of my response to Sam Harris's book, I once had occasion to drop in at Richard Dawkins's blog site and say a few things. I don't quite remember why I went there, but it was part of a general discussion. This involved reading some of the other posts, and it occurred to me that just because the famous atheist is an Oxford don doesn't keep his rank-and-file readers and commenters from being the kind of audience that Aquinas would not exactly envy. If careful and informed thought were a rich hardwood, we are talking oak veneer for the mobile home bathroom.

But Hitchens also has this complaint. It appears that the medieval period of faith built a bunch of imposing edifices, but do you know how they did it? "And also if humanity had not been compelled, on pain of extremely agonizing consequences, to pay the exorbitant tithes and taxes that raised the imposing edifices of religion" (65).

This is to be distinguished from the way we do it today. We enlightened modern ones pay virtually no taxes at all, and if we voluntarily opt out of the benign tax system of the modern state, nothing off-putting happens at all—perhaps a reasonable letter of sweet admonition from the head tax guy, reminding us in a friendly way that our government needs our continued voluntary compliance. But however firm his letter might be, there is certainly no hint of "extremely agonizing consequences." All the imposing edifices that *we* build are funded by car washes, bake sales, that kind of thing.

This is a chapter that is titled "The Metaphysical Claims of Religion Are False." Now with a title like that, one would expect a little argumentation (and, to be fair, there might be some in coming chapters), but here we find little more than what might be called the Argument for Infidelity from the *Bon Mot* (AIBM). Turns out that Laplace was one time talking with Napoleon, and when asked why the "figure of god did not appear in Laplace's mind-expanding calculations" (66–67), he replied with *"Je n'ai pas besoin de cette hypothese."* Well, you kind of had to have been there.

But Laplace's claim that he had no need of that hypothesis was still "cool, lofty, and considered" (67). God does not exist because one time a really smart guy unloaded a witticism on a general.

Hitchens denies that our awareness of the absence of God began at some dramatic moment

> such as Nietzsche's histrionic and self-contradictory pronouncement that god was dead. Nietzsche could no more have known this, or made the assumption that god had ever been alive, than a priest or witch doctor could ever declare that he knew god's will. (67)

What this shows, besides the fact that Hitchens doesn't understand Nietzsche at *all*, is that he *does* understand the presence of a rival, a real competitor. Nietzsche is one of those unbelievers who was quite capable of writing a compelling sentence, just like Hitchens. If it is true, as Joel McDurmon argues, that we are seeing *The Return of the Village Atheist*,[3] this is one of those cases where one gunslinger says to another that "This town's not big enough for the both of us." The opera of unbelief was not written for two sopranos.

---

3. Joel McDurmon, *The Return of the Village Atheist* (Powder Springs, GA: American Vision, 2007).

I said earlier that this chapter didn't really have any arguments, but that is not *quite* right. There is one, a cute little puppy:

> Thus the postulate of a designer or creator only rais-
> es the unanswerable question of who designed the
> designer or created the creator. Religion and theology
> and theodicy . . . have consistently failed to overcome
> this objection. (71)

The reason we can't overcome it is because it is not a proper objection. Unless there is a known principle excluding the eternality of anything at all, there could be no basis for such an objection. And were we to cook up such a principle, we would find that it excluded not only God, but the possibility of our having a universe at all. *Something* is eternal. That something is either God, as we believe, or it is matter, *stuff*, as Hitchens believes. If infinite regresses are incoherent, and any stopping point to head off that regress is always arbitrary by definition, then how'd we get here? Under the influence of various drugs, modern physicists have postulated the explosion of everything out of an "almost nothing," but their departmental supply offices have not been able to assemble enough drugs to get them to assert the primordial kablooey from *absolute* nothing. Yet. Anything but God.

> If one must have faith in order to believe something,
> or believe in something, then the likelihood of that
> something having any truth or value is considerably

diminished. The harder work of inquiry, proof, and demonstration is infinitely more rewarding, and has confronted us with findings more 'miraculous' and 'transcendent' than any theology. (71)

I swear, it's as though Hitchens has never even *heard* of epistemology. Over there, we have a bunch of dopes just *believing* stuff, while over here, under a florescent lab light, wearing our white lab coats, we just *know* things.

Although not in the sense intended, he is quite right that this is a "miraculous" and "transcendent" business. You see, Hitchens doesn't believe in things by faith. *He* just engages in the harder work of inquiry, proof, and demonstration. So, it would appear to me that he has faith in the efficacy of inquiry, proof, and demonstration. What is this faith based on? Well, Hitchens cannot answer the question because his faith in these things is so absolute that the question itself appears to him to be gibberish. It has never occurred to him that the process of reason can itself be examined and questioned. What are the preconditions of a reason that is reliable and trustworthy, and does Hitchens's materialistic conception of the universe provide us with those preconditions? Not even close.

Atoms bang around. Some of them bang around in my skull and generate feelings of love for Jesus Christ. Some others, doing exactly the same kind of thing, bounce around in Hitchens's skull and produce an opposing sentiment. Neither of us thinks the way he does because his claims are *true*, for pity's sake. There is no possible way to draw a correlation between my chemical reactions and the outside world, or his chemical reaction and the outside world. I type because my brain burbles. Why does Hitchens type? God only knows.

CHAPTER 5

MUCHO MACARONIC
MIRABILE DICTU

C hapter Six of Hitchens's book is all about "Arguments from Design." I have gone back and forth in my mind about how to approach this one. Should I do a slow, inexorable build to the point in my last paragraph where I place the capstone of a fun quotation from this chapter, doing so with loud whoops, or should I just start with that point? I decided to just start with it.

I am afraid that Hitchens does not really respect his creationist adversaries. He is glad that the courts have protected Americans from "the inculcation of compulsory 'creationist' stupidity in the classroom" (78). Now I understand a fierce uppercut, and I actually respect the ability to deliver one. But you really shouldn't *write* things like that, not in a chapter where you also (for inexplicable reasons) wrote something like the following: "We have only recently established that a cow is closer in family to a whale than to a horse; other wonders certainly await us" (94).

Well, on the principles that appear to be operating here, it certainly looks as though other wonders do promise to prance across the stage in front of us. This is the victory of vaudeville in the natural sciences. And this wonder, along with the next ones, *will* be inculcated in classrooms across America, with no judge available to snort rudely at them or declare them, if not unconstitutional, at least mildly amusing. But we do not dare to call this kind of thing compulsory stupidity, for it is a Decree of Science.

Proceeding to an actual argument, Hitchens attributes arguments from design to a universal solipsistic tendency among human beings to assume that they are being "waited on."

"The design arguments, which are products of this same solipsism, take two forms: the macro and micro" (77).

Our self-centeredness makes us think that it is "all about us." But, Hitchens argues, it is not all about us, because the planet where we live is just right for us. I know, but I am pretty sure that that is what he said.

This vanity allows us to overlook the implacable fact that, of the other bodies in our own solar system alone, the rest are all either far too cold to support anything recognizable as life, or far too hot. The same, as it happens, is true of our own blue and rounded planetary home, where heat contends with cold to make large tracts of it into useless wasteland, and where we have come to learn that we live, and have always lived, on a climatic knife edge. Meanwhile, the sun is getting ready to explode and devour its dependent planets like some jealous chief or tribal deity. Some design! (80)

So then, we live in a place well suited for life, and this is an argument against God putting us here because other places (where He didn't put us) are *not* well suited for us? I see. A housewife is taunted with incompetence because she keeps the toaster on the kitchen counter, where it works well, instead of in the toilet, where it wouldn't? But of course, that whole family *is* on a knife edge, for one day she might go nuts and throw it in the toilet (where scientists tell us it will not work well), and *then* where will our toast be? *Exactly*.

"Fish do not have fins because they need them for the water. It is exactly the other way about: a process of adaptation and selection" (78-79). What does Hitchens mean exactly by "the other way about?" How do you turn this sentence around? "Fish do not have fins because they need them for the water." Okay then. Why do they have them? I don't think he means to turn it around by giving another assigned reason—e.g., they need them for playing the guitar. He must mean that there is no *reason* they have them. They mutated a proto-fin which gave a small survival advantage, but the whole thing was blind, dumb luck. There is a reason why surviving fish have fins (fins helped them survive), but there is no reason related to them needing them for the water. I think that must be what he is saying, but it is a curious way of saying it. It seems to me that "fish have fins because they need them for the water" and "fish randomly developed fins because they provide a survival advantage in water" amount to the same thing. But I am a ignernt creationist, so what do I know?

Hitchens professes to have an open mind:

> Our side willingly concedes this point: we are prepared for discoveries in the future that will stagger our faculties even more than the vast advances in knowledge that have come to us since Darwin and Einstein. However, these discoveries will come to us in the same way—by means of patient and scrupulous and (this time, we hope) unfettered inquiry. (80-81)

Unfettered inquiry, aye. Hitchens has just finished chortling (exactly three pages earlier) about how the courts have protected Americans from hearing a dissenting viewpoint on the subject of design. Unfettered inquiry means (please allow me to translate) that there will be no *crazy* viewpoints that challenge the reigning orthodoxy. Other than *that*, the sky's the limit. For us to have unfettered discourse, we have to keep fettering these pesky creationists. Such is the price of true academic freedom.

But let us move on and talk about the evolution of the eye. We "evolved from sightless bacteria" (82). This is a huge big deal, and we ought to pay it the attention it deserves. "It is immensely fascinating and rewarding to know that at least forty different sets of eyes, and possibly sixty different sets, have evolved in quite distinct and parallel, if comparable, ways" (83).

Quoting Dr. Michael Shermer, Hitchens describes the long, torturous climb to the Rube Goldberg eyeball we all know and love. First a handful of light sensitive cells, then on to a recessed eyespot, then the deep recession eyespot, and then, *mirabile dictu*, a pinhole camera eye focusing images on the deeply-recessed layer of light-sensitive cells, and then, *mucho macaronic mirabile dictu*, a pinhole lens eye that can focus the image, and then on to the complex version found, for example, in my very own baby blues (82–83).

Heh. Just imagine (to take one example out of countless thousands) how many millions of years blind evolution spent in trying to get the placement of the first pinhole right. Doesn't even know that a pinhole could possibly be helpful, and, even though random mutation does serve up random pinholes from time to time (not to mention gaping holes), there is nothing to prevent it from placing the pinholes in places where they would be absolutely useless.

This is a good example of what Michael Behe means by irreducible complexity. In the long developmental journey from the first three light-sensitive cells to the eye of the osprey, what percentage of that time was the eye closed for remodeling (and therefore possessed of that condition that scientific laymen call *blindness*)? And during those periods of blindness, what evolutionary advantage was conferred such that the remodeling continued apace?

Nevertheless,

> The real 'miracle' is that we, who share genes with the original bacteria that began life on the planet, have evolved as much as we have. Other creatures did not develop eyes at all, or developed extremely weak ones. There is an intriguing paradox here: evolution does not have eyes but it can create them. (84)

Hitchens calls it a paradox when he is waving his hands over an incoherence, but is quite impatient when he thinks Christians are doing it. And he thinks we are doing it when we say that all-seeing God created the eye. No, he counters, trenchantly. *That* would have to have been done by a blind process. The blind leading the blind got us *out* of the evolutionary ditch.

"Why *do* people keep saying, 'God is in the details'? He isn't in ours, unless his yokel creationist fans wish to take credit for his clumsiness, failure and incompetence" (85). This is one place where a central problem of atheism (ingratitude) comes out with a vengeance. The apostle Paul says that the sinfulness of man is revealed in two central things—a refusal to honor God as God, and a refusal to give Him *thanks*. Ingratitude is the fountainhead of a lot of problems. In this case, Hitchens thinks that his body is an enormous bit of luck provided it was a sheer accident. But if it was designed by a loving Father in heaven, Hitchens wants to know where the complaint department is.

But shall the pot say to the potter, "Why did You make the handles like this?" Would not a far more graceful response be a simple *thank you*? Everyone one of us, every day, is standing under an enormous waterfall of cascading blessings. The fact that my ankles work, for example, and that my body is fighting off infection, and that my lunch tastes good, and the pleasure I get from a good sneeze, and the blessing of sleep (every night!), and the fact that I can see things (in *color*), and that . . . but I have to stop. I could spend the rest of my life writing about all the ways that God was good to me in the last fifteen minutes alone. This is, in my mind, a fundamental argument for the existence of the triune God of Scripture. Without Him, I have no one to thank. In Hitchens's worldview, he has no one to thank, but this appears to be the way he wants it.

But we must continue.

This is what makes piffle out of the ignorant creationist sneer, which compares evolution to a whirlwind
blowing through a junkyard of parts and coming up
with a jumbo jet. For a start, there are no "parts" lying
around waiting to be assembled. For another thing,
the process of acquisition and discarding of "parts"
(most especially wings) is as far from a whirlwind as
could conceivably be. The time involved is more like
that of a glacier than a storm. For still another thing,
jumbo jets are not riddled with non-working or su-
perfluous "parts" lamely inherited from less success-
ful aircraft. Why have we agreed so easily to call this
exploded old nontheory by its cunningly chosen new
disguise of "intelligent design"? (86-87)

Allow me to answer this paragraph in the brief com-
pass that it deserves. First, it is not an "ignorant"
creationist sneer—it is an illustration offered by Fred
Hoyle, not exactly your average creationist cornpone.
Second, the fact that the illustration has preassem-
bled parts was a way of giving evolution a head start
in the comparison. But okay, have it your way. Let's
have the whirlwind manufacture the parts too, just
like evolution had to. That any better? Third, slow-
ing the process down to glacier speeds makes things
worse for Mr. Hitchens, but I am happy to work with
it. Okay, let's have a glacier inch through the junkyard
and make us a plane. And last, the way Hitchens glibly
pronounces the body full of vestigial leftovers is something that the continued development of medical science should have taught us to quit doing. Ignorance

of function does not mean there is no function. As my wise grandmother used to say, "Never celebrate vestigialness prematurely."

Hitchens goes on to claim that "researchers were able to show how the nontheory of 'irreducible complexity' is a joke" (87). And he says this while not bothering to define irreducible complexity, and the behavior of proteins that he goes on to describe (as discovered by this study) has nothing to do with irreducible complexity, except, perhaps, as yet another *example* of it. A mechanism is irreducibly complex when the removal of any one part does not give you partial function, but rather *no* function. And what this means is that there is no evolutionary advantage in the manufacturing of parts individually—they confer no advantage until they are all assembled into the final functioning unit.

Hitchens then returns to his idea of Ockham's razor. "No divine plan, let alone angelic intervention, is required. *Everything works without that assumption*" (95, emphasis his).

The assumption he makes here in his application of "the simplest explanation is most likely" is that the elimination of God from the creation of all things is a simplifying move. It may have simplified Hitchens's personal life, but it most emphatically does not simplify our explanations of how spiders figured out web engineering. The fact that a story can be told without appeal to the divine purposes is a *simplistic* move, but that is not the same thing as a *simplifying* move. In fact, evolution requires us to gather an almost endless series of rocks in our pockets, and once we get past a certain point, we start to walk all crooked.

> What believers will do, now that their faith is optional and private and irrelevant, is a matter for them. We should not care, as long as they make no further attempt to inculcate religion by any form of coercion. (96)

What we really need here is a commitment from Hitchens to reject the inculcation of *any* worldview (secular or otherwise) through "any form of coercion." I could go for that. But I don't believe that a supporter of a tax-funded secular school system can really afford to make that move. A genuine free market of ideas (that included the schools) is a terrifying thought for them. It is one of the reasons we are seeing this rash of books from the atheist corner.

CHAPTER 6

THE NEED FOR HUMAN SACRIFICE

I think I will treat the next two chapters together. Chapter Seven of Hitchens's book is on the nightmare we call the Old Testament, and Chapter Eight informs us why "The 'New' Testament Exceeds the Evil of the 'Old' One."

That which is good in the Old Testament is, according to Hitchens, not unique to it.

> But however little one thinks of the Jewish tradition, it is surely insulting to the people of Moses to imagine that they had come this far under the impression that murder, adultery, theft, and perjury were permissible. (99)

But he forgets the heart of man, both ancient and modern. And I do not mean the heart of man in some hyperspiritualized sense, but rather the heart of man as indicated by what he actually does. In the world into which these commandments came, human sacrifice was not uncommon. Herodotus records how each Babylonian woman was required to do a "tour of duty" as a temple prostitute. As for theft, the distinctions between *meum* and *tuum* were particularly blurry, especially when dealing with the members of another tribe. The codification of these standards represented a true advance in civilized liberty.

But what about now?

To take just one example, does Hitchens seriously want to maintain that the evil of adultery is self-evident in our day? In the circles he travels in, is adultery *such* an evil that everyone recoils in horror from the news of yet another straying husband or wife? When a marriage cracks up because one of the partners was seeing someone on the side, what sort of comment might you hear from Hitchens at a Washington, D.C., cocktail party? "What Smith did is *reprehensible*. Why this is something that *Moses* didn't even need to tell his unwashed barbarian followers. Even *they* would know this was an evil and an outrage." As one of our prophets has put it, don't hold your breath.

Hitchens makes fun of the "insanely detailed regulations governing oxes that gore and are gored," along with "micromanagement of agricultural disputes" (100). This is not the heart of his argument at all— he is just setting the stage by showing how irreverent he can be—but it is kind of funny. Think about it. He is laughing at these rubes for micromanaging agriculture. He pokes fun at the ancient Hebrew predilection for "insanely detailed regulations." And where does Christopher Hitchens live? I believe I read somewhere that it is in the Washington, D.C., area, that vast and inexhaustible supply of micromanaging and insanely detailed regulations. The ancient Hebrews had Ten Commandments, and one slim volume of commentary on those commandments. Go to the nearest law library to you and ask to see the regulations that *you*, enlightened modern man, live under. They will show you shelf after shelf of big fat books, and the incoming regulations will, on a daily basis, far surpass the Mosaic code in volume. And what they overdo in quantity they will make up for in pettiness, hubris, and incoherence.

But then we get to his real objection to the Old Testament, which is moral.

> The Bible may, indeed does, contain a warrant for trafficking in humans, for ethnic cleansing, for slavery, for bride-price, and for indiscriminate massacre, but we are not bound by any of it because it was put together by crude, uncultured human mammals. (102)

Now, let me allow for the sake of argument that Hitchens has correctly read these passages. This is a big suppose, for he has done nothing of the kind, but let us grant it. Let us pretend that the Old Testament allows for all this stuff in just the way Hitchens supposes. And let us pretend further that it gives warrant for such practices *today*, provided you believe it. Now here is my question, directed against Hitchens's central objection. Given his atheism, what is wrong with any of this? This is what people do sometimes.

We are not bound to obey the Old Testament, he says, because it was put together by mammals. In the same way, we are not bound to Hitchens's book either, manufactured by mammals also. "Ah," he might say. "I said 'crude, uncultured mammals.'" And I would reply, "Exactly." Have you seen the size of the Department of Agriculture, and all their micromanaging regulations? They wrote a book, you wrote a book, there is no God over us, and so who cares?

We are not bound to the Old Testament, he says. But why, on his principles, are we bound to *reject* it? Why are we bound to *anything*?

"Intelligent schoolchildren have been upsetting their teachers with innocent but unanswerable questions ever since Bible study was instituted" (104). Yes, but this happens in Bible classes (routinely, I might add) because the kids asking the questions have a standard. Usually, the standard consists of principles they have learned elsewhere in the Bible, and their question is one of harmonization. How can God require this here when He required that over there? These are good questions, and they ought to be encouraged. But when someone rejects the whole business, one of the first things that should have occurred to him is that all right to ask all questions has evaporated. In order to bring a charge, you must have a standard. If there is no God, then what is that standard, and why is it obligatory? To this question, Hitchens has absolutely no answer.

And so, if the Old Testament is what he claims (it isn't) then I am the one who has a problem with it, *and he is the one who does not have a problem with it.*

But why is the New Testament worse? Why does the New Testament contain more evil? In the next chapter, he doesn't really address this question directly at all. He goes in for a goodish bit of various textual criticisms, not to mention giving an ear to gnostic counter-accounts, but this would simply make the New Testament unreliable, or contradictory.

> The contradictions and illiteracies of the New Testament have filled up many books by eminent scholars, and have never been explained by any Christian authority except in the feeblest terms of 'metaphor' and 'a Christ of faith.' (115)

This kind of confident pronouncement shows that Hitchens really doesn't get out much, and when he does, he rubs shoulders with the kind of Christians who lost their bearings seventy-five years ago. The contradictions "have never been explained" except in terms of metaphor, or the Christ of faith? That's the kind of answer you might get from an alcoholic Bible-as-lit professor who used to be a Methodist minister once. But for Christians who care about the inspiration and infallibility of Scripture, there is a minor industry producing apologetic materials addressing every Bible difficulty you might think of. Some of them are strained, some are hokey, some are wooden, and many are shrewd, scholarly, learned, and wise. But none of them, contra Hitchens, are nonexistent.

> The case of biblical consistency or authenticity or "inspiration" has been in tatters for some time, and the rents and tears only become more obvious with better research, and thus no 'revelation' can be derived from that quarter. So, then, let the advocates and partisans of religion rely on faith alone, and let them be brave enough to admit that this is what they are doing. (122)

Hitchens needs to come to the realization that, with this book, he is challenging Christians who believe the Bible and who will defend it. They will not defend it with vaporous appeals to fideism, but rather to the truth which can be objectively and genuinely known.

But I must say one thing about why Hitchens thinks the New Testament more evil than the Old. Remember, he has no basis for saying anything is evil, but he thinks he does. Apart from the chapter title, he does not make an explicit argument for the claim. But the implicit argument appears to be the fact that the New Testament defends the Old Testament, claiming to find in the death of Christ the complete fulfillment of all the sacrifices of the Old. This would include "almost" sacrifices, like that of Isaac by Abraham (109). And in this identification, Hitchens is quite correct. The Old Testament and the New stand or fall together.

But Hitchens has no basis for indignation about *anything*. And this is why he is required to sit quietly when I tell him that the Christian faith is a faith based on human sacrifice. We do not reject human sacrifice, but rather rejoice that the ultimate human sacrifice has been offered to God, and accepted by God, and that we have therefore been liberated from our sins. Apart from human sacrifice, there is no remission of sins.

Hitchens rejects human sacrifice out of sheer personal prejudice. There are no standards, there is no God, people do things and that's one of them, and why should anybody obey a standard based on what creeps Hitchens out? I reject any further human sacrifice because the perfect sacrifice was offered on the cross two thousand years ago. We are all invited to submit to that sacrifice, accepting it, and, when we do, God accepts us. If we reject God, as Hitchens has done, we reject the ability to reject anything.

If this reality-therapy is pressed on the atheist (as it needs to be), it will perhaps quiet the room for a moment. And in that silence, the only thing that needs to be said is that God was in Christ, reconciling the world to Himself. We declare *the* human sacrifice—Christ and Him crucified.

CHAPTER 7

SOME PRAISE FOR HITCHENS

I live in the northern portion of Idaho, in the part that looks like a rock chimney. I bring this up merely to lend credence to my next claim, which is that the lakes up here are pretty cold year-round. When you are swimming or waterskiing, even in August, you are always in for a *bracing* experience. And I bring that up because occasionally, while floating around in the water with your skis on, you will float into a nice warm spot. Ah, you think, and then it is over. But it is really nice while it lasts.

The next chapter by Hitchens is that nice warm spot. I agreed with virtually everything he said, and that is because Chapter Nine is on the Koran. Now, of course,

I exclude the occasional asides about the Christian faith that he offers. And we also have to keep in mind the fact that if Islam really *were* the true religion of God, Hitchens would still be attacking it, although presumably for alternative reasons. Someone with a large vocabulary is never without a rock to throw, so long as he has a mind to throw it.

With that said, I agreed with most of what he wrote here. And that leads to another point, which is one of respect for Hitchens. We live in a time where it takes courage to speak the truth about Islam. For much of this book, Hitchens has been the bad boy in the mandatory Bible class in a parochial junior high school, embarrassing the teacher with questions and shocking the cute girls.

But when he takes on Islam this way, he is doing something that takes genuine courage. The previous two chapters, where he said a number of outrageous things about the Christian faith, will not, under any conceivable set of circumstances cause the Baptists of Little Rock to riot and burn down the city. Neither will Jerry Falwell issue a fatwa, offering a sure ticket to heaven for anyone who bumps off Hitchens. True, it *is* possible that Pat Robertson might prophesy that a meteor will land on Hitchens's car, with him in it, but this sort of thing from Robertson can scarcely be reckoned as a real threat. If he were to make such a statement, I would be happy to ride around with Hitchens in his car for the day, and I have to confess that I would feel perfectly safe.

But militant Islam is very much present in the modern world, and it is a toxic and murderous faith. They have threatened and conducted murder for offenses in the same league as those committed in this chapter—think of Salman Rushdie, the Danish cartoons, etc. Hitchens must know this, which means that for all his posturing and thin argumentation, he is not a poser. He is not pretending to bet—he actually has some chips on the table. This is not an instance of damning with faint praise. I am praising his courage, not the fact that he frequently talks nonsense in elegant prose.

CHAPTER 8

ON MULBERRY STREET

I
n the first place, I think there must have been an editorial mishap in the assigned title of Hitchens's next chapter. It was "The Tawdriness of the Miraculous and the Decline of Hell." The chapter is about the former, and not about the latter at all. I can only conjecture that it was at one time going to be a longer chapter, but events intervened as they so often do. This being the case, I will not undertake here to answer Hitchens on the question of Hell since the decline of Hell has apparently had a corresponding decline in comments made about it by Hitchens in this chapter.

But Hitchens *does* object to tawdry miracles, again on the basis of Ockham's razor. The particular application of that razor is this time brought to us courtesy of

David Hume. If you think you have witnessed a miracle, there are two possibilities.

> The first is that the laws of nature have been suspended (in your favor). The second is that you are under a misapprehension, or suffering from a delusion. Thus the likelihood of the second must be weighed against the likelihood of the first And if you are separated from the "sighting" by many generations, and have no independent corroboration, the odds must be adjusted still more drastically. (141)

I actually think the winnowing process here, as stated, is quite reasonable. But there is a hidden worldview assumption tucked away here, one that needs to be brought out into the open. If you are the kind of person who believes that the likelihood of miracles is precisely zero (because of a previous commitment to materialism), then you will automatically assume that you were mistaken or deluded. You never even have to go check. "Can't happen." But if you are the kind of person who finds pictures of the Blessed Virgin in your bathroom mold, or (for gullible Protestants) an image of Billy Graham on the tortilla, then your problem is easily resolved the other way. "It's a sign!" But if you believe that miracles are possible but rare, then you will proceed with caution—disbelieving most accounts of miracles, but not all of them.

One of the miracles that all genuine Christians affirm is the miracle of the Resurrection, and I am grateful that Hitchens spends some time on this—and not

just on the kind of miracles that could be easily re-
produced by a half competent stage magician. But in
his discussion of the Resurrection, he says something
astonishing.

> For now, and on a review even of the claims made by
> the faithful, one can say that resurrection would not
> prove the truth of the dead man's doctrine, nor his
> paternity, nor the probability of still another return
> in fleshly or recognizable form. (143)

In other words, Christopher Hitchens does not believe that Jesus came back from the dead but, just to
be sure, he wants to make it clear that even if Jesus
did conquer death, he, Hitchens, wants to reserve the
right to continue in his unbelief. This is deep-rooted
unbelief. No, it is more than unbelief—it is defiance.
And it is the same kind of unbelief that we see in the
resurrection accounts in the Gospels. The first group
to know of the Resurrection were the guards posted at the tomb, and the second group were the men
who had had Christ killed in the first place. They then
bribed the guards to lie about what had happened. In
other words, they *knew* Christ had risen, just as He had
declared that He would, and they were *still* opposed
to Him. The third group to know of the Resurrection
were Christ's women disciples, and the fourth group,
bringing up the rear, were the male disciples. Hitchens
is quite right here. Knowledge of the Resurrection
does not amount to faith in the one who rose. That

kind of faith is a gift from Heaven, and it is a gift that only God can give.

> Having no reliable or consistent witnesses, in any-
> thing like the time period needed to certify such ex-
> traordinary claims, we are finally entitled to say that
> we have a right, if not an obligation, to respect our-
> selves enough to disbelieve the whole thing. (143)

There is another hidden assumption here. Hitchens wants "reliable or consistent witnesses." But if there were witnesses to Christ's Resurrection who did *not* then follow Him, in what sense can they be called reliable? And if they did follow Him and added the voice of their witness to the five hundred who saw the ris-en Lord, this would give Hitchens a basis for dismiss-ing them—they are obvious partisans now. In other words, he wants an objective witness, the kind who would testify that Jesus rose from the dead, while re-fusing at the same time to worship Him. But that kind of "objectivity" is not available when we come to the Resurrection. Those who knew of the Resurrection but did not have corresponding faith in Christ had every motive to lie about it. And those who submitted to Him as the Son of God (Rom. 1:4) would not be con-sidered "objective" as far as Hitchens is concerned.

With that, Hitchens then launches into a discus-sion of various "tawdry" miracles and, just as with the chapter on Islam, I found myself largely agreeing with him here. Talking about the kind of miracle popular in

Roman Catholic circles, Hitchens says, "Extend this to the present day, where the statues of virgins or saints are sometimes said to weep or bleed" (144). I was reminded of the time, years ago, when I was reading through Augustine's *City of God*, and had the enjoyable sensation of seeing that august church father mocking the *faux* miracles of paganism. If I remember correctly, his example was a statue of Apollo that wept. There is a certain kind of miracle that is just the kind of thing that a carnal heart would think up, and this kind of weeping, bleeding miracle fits that description.

But one of the most striking things about the Gospel accounts (when compared to other ancient writings about Jesus) is the strict economy of miracles. Many religious writers, once they warm to their subject, appear to subscribe to the view that if one's good, two's better. Now the miraculous cannot be removed from orthodox Christianity and, as Hitchens appears to acknowledge, the central event of the Resurrection is a nonnegotiable item for all faithful Christians. But at the same time, it is striking how the other miracles that Christ performed are held, as it were, close to the chest. They are not soft-pedaled or denied, but they are definitely held in their appropriate place. "A wicked and adulterous generation seeketh after a sign."

Carnal stories of the miraculous are the religious equivalent of Dr. Seuss's *And to Think That I Saw It on Mulberry Street*. Hitchens is perfectly within his rights to object to these, and I share his objection. But he is wrong to confound the wonder-a-minute crowd with the judicious confirmation of claims to divine authority found in Scripture. I wouldn't want to listen to anybody speak to me in the name of God without "seeing his papers." Doing in the name of God what only God can do (and not what a stage magician could do) is the signature at the bottom of those papers (2 Cor. 12:12).

Just as an aside, Hitchens throws into this discussion of the miraculous a different matter altogether, which is the ministerial interpretation of providential circumstances. If a calamity or disaster is said to be the result of a particular sin, this does not involve the miraculous at all. A man reaps what he sows, and the same thing goes for nations. It is the role of the Church to call the nation to repentance, and for preachers to interpret certain disasters as judgments (Katrina, 9-11, etc.) is not a bogus use of their authority, and it is not an appeal to the miraculous. Such connections could be silly (Katrina was a judgment on our nation because God was angry about the sloppy referees in the Super Bowl), or they could be judicious observations (Katrina was a judgment on a city built well below sea level in hurricane country, which city thought it a good idea to try to govern its affairs through corruption, drunkenness, perversion, and vice). But even if such a connection were made erroneously, it would not be an example of an appeal to the miraculous.

I was grateful for a couple of things in this chapter, so let me finish with some comments on those. One was minor and the other more significant. The first is that, in a passing illustration, Hitchens allows that the seventeenth Earl of Oxford was the true author of the plays attributed to Shakespeare. The more of that kind of thing the better. Joe Sobran convinced me of this years ago.

> It does not matter to me whether Homer was one person or many, or whether Shakespeare was a secret Catholic or a closet agnostic. I should not feel my own world destroyed if the greatest writer about love and tragedy and comedy and morals was finally revealed to have been the Earl of Oxford all along. (150)

Now I won't go into all the reasons for thinking this, but let me test the limits of Hitchens's charity on this one. There is *also* good reason for believing that Edward de Vere, seventeenth Earl of Oxford, was the secret author of the Martin Marprelate tracts. And if you take these two data together, this means that the "greatest writer about love and tragedy and comedy and morals" was actually, at least in the late 1580s, one of the rowdiest Puritans ever. Now *there's* a fun thought experiment, one that I am currently pursuing in the form of an article that I am sure no one will ever publish.[4]

---

4. No one else, that is. We did, in fact, publish it in *Credenda/Agenda*, volume 20, issue 3, and you can read it via the magic of the Internet Archive at https://tinyurl.com/MartinShakespearePuritan.

The more significant acknowledgment from Hitchens follows just after this.

> But there is a great deal to be learned and appreciated from the scrutiny of religion, and one often finds oneself standing atop the shoulders of distinguished writers and thinkers who were certainly one's intellectual and sometimes even one's moral superiors. Many of them, in their own time, had ripped away the disguise of idolatry and paganism, and even risked martyrdom for the sake of disputes with their own co-religionists. (151)

This tone, had it prevailed throughout, would have been far more fitting in a book challenging religion. But Hitchens actually can't afford even this much, because it is a tone (even in this short section) that contradicts the thesis of the book, which is that religion poisons everything. Not only would the tone of the book be improved, so would the accuracy. Hitchens points here to the kind of gullibility that makes hucksterism in religious affairs so easy, and he is right to do so. In the high middle ages, there were enough pieces of the Virgin Mary's veil on display in the holy places of Europe to make a tent for Barnum and Bailey. And anybody who is too pious to find this funny has the kind of piety that always gives the Christian faith a bad name. A certain kind of piety gives the Gentiles occasion to blaspheme. The mind-numbing credulity that afflicts a certain kind of Christian reminds me of the justice in Oscar Wilde's comment that anybody who could read about the death of Little Nell in *The Old Curiosity Shop* without laughing must have a heart of stone. There are plenty of miraclemongers who are doing their thing in the name of Jesus, and they deserve everything that Hitchens can deliver to them, and they deserve it good and hard. But as Hitchens acknowledges here briefly, and should do so far more extensively, this is the same kind of critique of gullibility that is found in John Calvin's *Inventory of Relics*. When Hitchens comes to attack this kind of credulity and hypocrisy, he finds that many Christians have preceded him.

CHAPTER 9

YOU HAVE TO LEAVE
WICHITA TOO

As we continue through this book, it is becoming more and more apparent that Hitchens's gods—Science and Reason—are really starting to let him down.

In the previous chapter, Hitchens said in passing that "the 'Argument from Authority' is the weakest of all arguments" (150). And how do you know *that*? Well, science has shown, as reported in *All Scholars Review* . . . I am being facetious here, but the central point is a serious one. Far from being the weakest argument, all human knowledge of any kind whatever is dependent in significant ways upon the voice of authority. Hitchens pretends that this is not so by subsuming examples of *his* dependence on authority under the heading of "what everyone knows." Everyone knows the earth goes around the sun, even though neither Hitchens nor I have seen it. We both read it in a book published by the authorities. I am not disputing this, incidentally . . . I have a higher view of arguments from authority than Hitchens does. But he really needs to admit that science is his authority, not his personal method for finding everything out.

But Reason is the other god that is failing. This chapter in on religion's corrupt beginnings, meaning that all religions bear "the stamp of their origin." I want to ask you to join me as we look at the *structure* of Hitchens's argument here. Bear in mind that this is the structure of an argument crafted by a man who believes, really believes, in reason.

Here's how he goes: "Thus, if we watch the process of a religion in its formation, we can make some assumptions about the origins of those religions that were put together before most people could read" (155).

Hitchens then picks three examples—South Pacific cargo cults, the antics of a huckster evangelist named Marjoe, and the formation of Mormonism. Now with these three examples I quite agree with Hitchens that the cargo cults are sad, the hucksterism is appalling, and the historical tenets of Mormonism are beyond ridiculous. I also think that the structure of Hitchens's argument in this chapter is beyond ridiculous.

If his thesis were that there is no such thing as a genuine Federal Reserve Note, and debate arose over it, he could not make his case by saying that all pieces of green paper with currency values on them are counterfeit. "We can verify this by considering three examples of counterfeiters who were recently apprehended."

He then makes his strawman approach even more glaring by picking, as examples of counterfeiting, black and white xerox copies of money, the first attempt by an incompetent forger now serving five to ten, and a picture of a twenty dollar bill drawn by his nephew with an orange crayon. If he points to these transparent attempts, he cannot say something like, "what more do you need?" This is not the voice of reason; it is the intrusion of what logicians call informal fallacies.

One other thing. Near the conclusion of this chapter, he sets himself up in a big way when he gets to speculating about the motives of these religious charlatans.

> What interests me and always has is this: Do the preachers and prophets also believe, or do they too just "believe in belief"? Do they ever think to themselves, this is too easy. And do they then rationalize the trick by saying that either (a) if these wretches weren't listening to me they'd be in even worse shape; or (b) that if it doesn't do them any good then it still can't be doing them much harm? (165)

There is a third option. Suppose one of them, on holiday from haranguing the faithful, met Hitchens at a freethinkers conference. "What are you doing here?"

would be the obvious question. "Oh, I don't believe any of that stuff," came the cheerful reply. "I don't believe in God."

"But, but . . ."

"Look, I read your book, and I took special note of your question on page 165. There is a third option, beyond your (a) and (b). And here it is—(c) because these people are morons, they are too stupid to catch me, and because there is no God, I will not be caught in any stinkin' afterlife. In fact, there is no such thing as 'catching anybody.' The money's good, indoor job, no heavy lifting. You *do* agree with me that there is no afterlife? Good . . . ho, ho, ho! What a racket, eh? How's *your* racket going?"

"But reason, science . . . collective good, ethics . . . ," Hitchens trails off.

"Look, friend," our atheist Elmer Gantry says, "you can't leave Kansas without leaving Wichita too."

CHAPTER 10

IN THE NAME OF REASON

I n chapter twelve, Hitchens stops arguing fallaciously from the presumed origin of all religions, and argues briefly, but equally fallaciously,
from the collapse of religious movements. He makes
this case on the basis of the collapse of one religious
movement.

"It can be equally useful and instructive to take a
glimpse at the closing of religions, or religious movements" (169). He does this by examining the religious
hysteria that accompanied the rise and fall of Sabbatai
Sevi, a false messiah among the Jews in the mid-sev-
enteenth century. There was quite a hubbub for a time,
and then the whole thing cratered.

There is an Indian tribe in our neck of the woods named the Nez Perce, which is also the name of the county immediately to the south of us. The name was given by French explorers, and it means "pierced nose." The problem is that the Nez Perce did not have pierced noses. The misnomer perhaps came from the fact that the French encountered an early North American hippie, an outcast from the tribe, a loner who liked to listen to the voices in his head. *He* had a pierced nose, and the French may have had the same reasoning methods of Hitchens: "Find a sample size of one, and render general by induction."

Remember, of course, that we are getting this treatment in the name of *reason*.

CHAPTER 11

STALIN HAS NO GOD, INCLUDING HITCHENS

T he next chapter in *God is Not Great* asks the question "Does Religion Make People Behave Better?" We have noted before that the question is framed improperly. It is like asking "Does Anything Going by the Name of Medical Treatment Cure Cancer?" Well, some things do and most don't. The world is not the simple place that most atheists would like to have it be.

But although the title of this chapter asks the question the wrong way, the text of this chapter was significantly more tolerable than some of his other tirade chapters. In this chapter, Hitchens shows himself capable of considerable nuance, and he raises the *central* question in all atheism/problem of evil discussion, which we will get to shortly. He also shows himself capable of greatly admiring people who do not share his atheism at all. But sometimes he admires the wrong thing.

For example, Hitchens admires the courage and moral impact of Martin Luther King Jr., and he does so with his eyes open—there is great admiration here, but no prim hagiography. Speaking of King, he says,

> This does not in the least diminish his standing as a great preacher, any more than does the fact that he was a mammal like the rest of us, and probably plagiarized his doctoral dissertation, and had a notorious fondness for booze and for women a good deal younger than his wife. He spent the remainder of his last evening in orgiastic dissipation, for which I don't blame him. (176)

Hitchens's broadmindedness here would probably not be extended to James Dobson, if he were given to comparable behaviors, so we can only wonder about the principles of selection that are operative here. Nevertheless, Hitchens talks about a number of people who have made a difference in the world, including King, Lincoln, Gandhi, William Lloyd Garrison, and John Paul II. Some of them, he argues, made a difference in spite of their Christianity (King), some made a difference despite theological ambiguities (Lincoln), and some were well-intentioned types who only got underfoot (Gandhi). But, he argues, pound for pound, the secularists have a better record.

> The worse the offender, the more devout he turns out to be. It can be added that some of the most dedicated relief workers are also believers (though as it happens the best ones I have met are secularists who were not trying to proselytize for any faith). (192)

Speaking of the fight against racism against in the American South, he says,

> Anybody, therefore, who uses the King legacy to justify the role of religion in public life must accept all the corollaries of what they seem to be implying. Even a glance at the whole record will show, first, that person for person, American freethinkers and agnostics and atheists come out the best. (180)

And he notes the time a Christian relief worker did not just blow off his question about this issue. "To my surprise, he did not dismiss my question. All that a missionary could do was to try and show people a different face of Christianity" (189).

The problem with this is that the setup is highly selective, and it is not surprising that it produces the desired results. For example, in this chapter Hitchens acknowledges that "many of King's inner circle and entourage were secular Communists and socialists" (179–180). They were helping to train brave volunteers like Mrs. Rosa Parks, and so on. But in the course of twentieth century, the Communists managed to execute or starve to death a minimum of *eighty-five million people*. This was managed in no small part due to the labors, excuses, and lies of their fellow travelers over here. What was the role of American freethinkers, agnostics, and atheists if we move out of the Western Hemisphere, away from the insult of separate drinking fountains, and we bring in the issues of the Gulag or the killing fields? What do we say about those who averted their eyes and did everything in their power to keep anybody else from trying to help those shut away in that monstrosity, that global evil?

In a previous chapter, Hitchens confessed his earlier fling with Marxism, but we have to remember that this was not just a matter of what ideas you might have been thinking in your youthful head. People were being slaughtered by the million over *there*, and they had their apologists over *here*. So let us ask hard questions across the board. I grant that a freethinker in Alabama was far *less* likely to support the pettiness of Jim Crow than a conservative Christian in that same state. I grant it, and it is an embarrassment to me. But that same freethinker was far *more* likely to make pathetic excuses for Mao than that very same conservative Christian. Is *that* an embarrassment to Hitchens? I hope so, and to include *all* the genocides of the twentieth century in this equation changes the discussion completely. Hitchens accuses the Vatican of conniving at the massacres of Rwanda (193). Were there any genocides in the twentieth century that *atheists* planned, executed, and defended? To ask the question is to answer it.

Two issues from this chapter remain. Here, as throughout this book, Hitchens is very free with his moral judgments. Speaking of King, he says "the filthy injustice of racism must be borne no longer" (173). He speaks of one outrage in the Rwandan massacre as "this ineffaceable crime" (192). It is very clear that Hitchens feels the outrage he expresses. But the one thing that he will not do is give us an accounting of that outrage. He gives us his sentiment. He cannot give us a *reason*, because he doesn't have one.

"No supernatural force was required to make the case against racism" (180). *That* sounded very confident. No transcendent reality is necessary in order for us to just know that to despise another human being on the basis of his race is objectively wrong and evil. Okay, then. We have now banished all talk of supernatural forces, angels, demons, the gospel, and the Holy Ghost. They are gone from the discussion. We have gathered in our chairs to hear Hitchens give the lecture that he now needs to deliver. The flyer caught my attention the moment I saw it. "The Atheistic Basis for Moral Absolutes." I am all ears, and I am actually starting to fidget in my seat. In a world where we can speak confidently of ineffaceable crimes, and filthy injustice, and in that same world where supernaturalism is unnecessary in making the case against racism . . .

well, then, let's hear it. Lay out the premises of your vaunted atheism, and then draw your objective moral conclusions from it. I hope they left time for a question and answer session. The last issue is one that I covered in my reply to Sam Harris. Hitchens makes the same mistake that Harris does, which is to represent us as saying that atheists are raving libertines. There is no god, and so let us debauch everything and everyone. But atheists are at great pains to show that they are as moral as the next guy, as Hitchens does in this chapter.

> But where would people be without faith? Would they not abandon themselves to every kind of license and selfishness? Is it not true, as G.K. Chesterton once famously said, that if people cease to believe in god, they do not believe in nothing but in anything? (184)

Hitchens recounts a debate between a Bishop Butler and A.J. Ayer, in which the good bishop said that he did not see why Ayer, given his atheism, did not live a life of "unbridled immorality" (185). "Was he in fact not telling Ayer, in his own naive way, that if freed from the restraints of doctrine *he himself* would choose to lead 'a life of unbridled immorality'? One naturally hopes not" (186).

The central critique here is not that all atheists are ready to burst forth into unrestrained licentiousness given the slightest provocation. Many atheists, atheism and all, don't want to be raving criminals, and that just is fine with me. I am not saying Hitchens is a serial murderer, or that he ought to be. I am not saying that civilized atheists are just pretending to be ethical. I know that Hitchens expresses genuine moral outrage, and I am glad that he does. It shows that he still is carrying the image of God, just as his name still marks him as a Christ-bearer. If he was baptized, he is carrying that as well.

This critique is not aimed at his *un*righteousness, but rather at his unsupported *self*-righteousness. The issue is not what Hitchens himself wants to do, but whether he can get his god Reason to rebuke a completely different atheist who was more of Stalin's frame of mind. The issue is not that atheism *requires* an atheist to starve millions in Georgia. It does not, so Hitchens doesn't have to. But it *does* necessitate that consistent atheists stand by mute, with nothing whatever to say, when others (theists and atheists alike) make choices that they *personally* would consider abominable and outrageous. This is because Stalin had no god, *including Hitchens*. The disapproval of Jehovah meant nothing to him, and the disapproval of Hitchens would have meant just as little. And Hitchens has no reason whatever that could possibly make Stalin see it differently. That is the issue. It is not whether Hitchens is Stalin. Of course he is not. The issue is whether Hitchens has anything whatever to say when Stalin is being Stalin. And he does not.

So whenever Hitchens condemns the moral behavior of anyone else, he is not proving that atheists can be moral too. He is proving, instead, that he is incapable of following his own premises out to the end of the road he is on. He is proving that he is blissfully unaware of the blatant contradictions in his system. No one can impose their morality on another, but then Hitchens begins dispensing moral judgments on others, and he does so with a snow shovel. This critique is directed at an *intellectual* failure of atheism, not at a moral failure. The subject is morality, but the failure is a failure in reason. This is unfortunate for them because it is a failure of their god.

CHAPTER 12

ONLY WRONG WHEN THE BUDDHISTS DO IT

At first glance, it may appear that the next chapter of Hitchens's book would be another one where there is considerable agreement. It is entitled "There Is No 'Eastern' Solution," and, of course, I completely agree with that, as far as it goes. In addition, I agree with Hitchens's assessment of *why* many Westerners have gone the guru route. It appears to be the same motive that persuades a foolish woman to try to clean her living room by rearranging the furniture, or a foolish student to try to improve his grades by buying additional notebook dividers. It promises change without actually delivering it.

But Hitchens says a few things in passing about rationality and argument that I really should respond to.

> But an extraordinary number of people appear to believe that the mind, and the reasoning faculty—the only thing that divides us from our animal relatives—is something to be distrusted and even, as far as possible, dulled. (198)

As a Christian, I agree with him that the mind is not to be rejected as it is in the East. We are commanded to love the Lord our God with all our *minds* as well as the rest of our beings. So Hitchens is not like a Zen master—he does not disparage reason, but rather praises it. But like the ancient Israelites condemned by Isaiah, his practice does not live up to his praise. The goddess Reason could, with good reason, say, "He draws near me with his mouth, and with his lips does honour me, but he has removed his heart far from me."

Hitchens quotes the Reginald Heber, the Anglican bishop of Calcutta and author of "Holy, Holy, Holy," and dismisses him as exhibiting the "condescension of old colonial boobies" (199). The first funny thing here is that Hitchens accused someone *else* of condescension, and in such a manner as to suggest that he believes condescension to be a negative trait. I had not detected this sentiment earlier in the book. But the second funny thing is that he quoted an offensive hymn from Heber, the bad parts being a statement that in that part of the world "only man is vile," followed up in the next verse with the statement that "The heathen in his blindness bows down to wood and stone." After Hitchens quotes this and has us join him in a good laugh at the bishop's expense, he proceeds to a detailed discussion that reveals that Bishop Heber was entirely correct in his evaluation of his surroundings. This is *reason?*

Hitchens accuses eastern mysticism of certain faults that are certainly faults, but he does not appear to realize that he is doing the very same things himself.

"They consist, like most professions of faith, in merely *assuming* what has to be proved" (202). Exactly so. This shows that Hitchens knows that *petitio principii* is a fallacy, which means that when asked to address how authoritative reason and logic are possible products of those chemical vats that we call brains, he needs to do more than blithely *assume* the role of reason and logic. He must account for them. And at some level, he knows that he has to do this—yet he still declines. Far easier to attack the Buddhists for doing it.

Another example. After discussing the Buddhist role in recruiting *kamikaze* pilots in WWII, Hitchens goes on to say this:

> Although many Buddhists now regret that deplorable attempt to prove their own superiority, no Buddhist since then has been able to demonstrate that Buddhism *was wrong in its own terms*. A faith that despises the mind and the free individual, that preaches submission and resignation, and that regards life as

a poor and transient thing, is *ill-equipped for self-criti-cism.* (204, emphasis mine)

This citation proves that he understands the con-cept of self-evaluation. Not all Buddhists want to re-cruit young pilots to become suicide pilots. But some clearly did, and Hitchens is here stating that, *given the premises,* those who did not wish to do this had *noth-ing to say* to those who did. This is almost a Euclidian parallel to the argument against atheism that I am pre-senting here. I grant that Hitchens doesn't want to run off and do whatever evil thing has been done by any other given atheists, as they have acted out *their* own sense of freedom, but the point is that Hitchens has nothing whatever to say to those who apply the prem-ises of atheism differently *and far more consistently.* He pretends that this is not checkmate, and he does this because he is ill-equipped for self-criticism.

CHAPTER 13

THE TEMPLE FIRES ARE
EXTINGUISHED

I n his next chapter, Hitchens takes on religion as
original sin. In this chapter, he demonstrates that
he understands the Christian gospel better than
many televangelists do, but his understanding is suf-
fused with the kind of hatred that brings a different
kind of confusion.

Hitchens says here that the behavior of various re-
ligionists is sometimes "exemplary," but that certain
foundational tenets of religion are "positively immoral" (205). He lists five such tenets:

- Presenting a false picture of the world to
the innocent and the credulous

195

- The doctrine of blood sacrifice
- The doctrine of atonement
- The doctrine of eternal reward and/or punishment
- The imposition of impossible tasks and rules (205)

He deals with the first of these in passing because it has been previously covered in the book. "All the creation myths of all people have long been known to be false, and have fairly recently been replaced by infinitely superior and more magnificent explanations" (205).

Well, *magnificent* is one word that comes to mind. One day there was almost-mathematical-point-nothing, and then it blew up. There was a problem in the reactors I believe. There was a lot of hydrogen involved, which eventually turned into Ralph Nader, the Dalai Lama, and Paris Hilton. If you doubt this compelling science, you need to subscribe to *National Geographic* and watch more of the Discovery Channel.

With regard to his fourth and fifth objections, it is not necessary to spend a great deal of time with them. As earlier, he mentions eternal punishment, but does not really develop his objections. There is not enough there to engage with. And as for his last objection, it seems to me that to be told to stay away from one tree in the world does not fit my definition of "an impossible task."

But that is all right. The heart of this chapter, and the heart of the issue between us, is the matter of human blood sacrifice and substitutionary atonement. And on this, the central issue, Hitchens writes with clarity and force, and shows that, despite his best efforts, he is perilously close to the kingdom, and needs to watch his step. "Before monotheism arose, the altars of primitive society reeked of blood, much of it human and some of it infant" (206). This is very true. And this was not unique to paganism. Hitchens brings up the story of Abraham, which, rightly understood, is a glorious one.

> There is no softening the plain meaning of this frightful story . . . . At the last available moment his hand was stayed, not by god as it happens, but by an angel, and he was praised from the clouds for showing his sturdy willingness to murder an innocent in expiation of his own crimes. (206–207)

Hitchens says rightly that there is no honest softening of this story. But there are some clarifications, corrections, and additions that make the story *more* potent, not less. So let me reassure Hitchens of what I am *not* trying to do. This is a story about human sacrifice, and I am not about to try to explain that away. To do so would be to try to explain away our only hope and glory.

That said, there is no indication that Abraham was offering Isaac up as a guilt offering for sins that Abraham had committed. It was more likely an ascension offering—representing entire consecration to God. At the same time, it *was* a type of *the* guilt offering—of course the death of Christ was the antitype. Abraham was told to take his son, his only son, and offer him up. The echoes of Christ as the only Son of God are unmistakable. In addition, Abraham traveled with Isaac a great distance to get to the place where God required it to be done—the region of Moriah. This was the *same place* where, almost two thousand years later, Christ was offered up as the supreme (and final) human sacrifice.

And last, the test here was not of Abraham's love for God—"Do you love me enough to kill your son?" As Hitchens recognizes, this would be a macabre test of love. The test was of Abraham's *faith*. God had told Abraham explicitly that his descendants would be as the stars in the sky, and that they would be reckoned *through Isaac*. Abraham therefore knew that Isaac was coming back down off the mountain with him. This was not only a type of the Crucifixion, it was a type of the Resurrection also. Abraham knew this, although he was mistaken in one detail. He thought Isaac was *actually* going to be raised up again from the dead (Heb. 11:18–19), when God had determined that he was to be "raised" up again, raised up alive from the altar. But in either case, Abraham knew that Isaac was going to come down off the mountain alive with him. That is what he told the servants, in faith. We will go to that mountain and worship, and then *we* will return to you. The test was of his faith, not of his love.

I said a moment ago that human sacrifice is not unique to paganism. The Christian faith is a faith that centers on human sacrifice. Other ancient religions did the same. But there is a key difference between pagan mythology and the Christian story in this regard. Paganism sacrifices humans and sublimates the whole thing—drawing the necessary benefit from the sacrifice while desiring to avoid ongoing explicit acknowledgment of what they are actually doing. A veil of edifying mythologies is always drawn over the founding murder and the sustaining sacrificial murders. Because of this, the cycle of sacrificial violence never ends— the idol is never satisfied for long, and because sins are never taken away for good, the idol always demands fresh blood.

The Christian faith declares a gospel that is the opposite of this. It is not opposite because there is no human sacrifice. Rather it is opposite because the sacrifice is preached to the world as an open scandal. There are no edifying lies. A veil is *not* drawn over it. The bloody violence is there for the world to see, and God has required us to preach this message (without tidying it up) until the end of the world. When we tell ourselves the truth about the need for human sacrifice, human sacrifices end. When we lie about the need for human sacrifice, wanting instead a more uplifting religion, the carnage is ongoing.

I think that Hitchens instinctively understands this. He tells a story about murder from the contemporary Middle East (207–208) which shows he understands that any murder in the name of religion *is the same thing as ancient blood sacrifice.* "The curse of Abraham continues to poison Hebron, but the religious warrant for blood sacrifice poisons our entire civilization" (208). This is a very important point. I think that Hitchens would agree that it is sublimated human sacrifice, but it does display the deep, driving need that mankind has for blood atonement. Men need it so badly that they will generate crusade after crusade, which consistently end in mass graves. But the reason for this is *not* that men are inspired by Abraham's prefiguring of the sacrifice to end all sacrifices. It is because, like Hitchens, they are refusing to look straight on at the death of Christ for the sins of the world. When the wracked body of Christ on the cross is truly *seen*, this is the completion and end of all our vain attempts to save ourselves through blood.

The choice between faith and unbelief is not a choice between nonviolence and violence. It is between violence unveiled and violence veiled. It is between sufficient sacrifice and *insufficient* sacrifice. It is the difference between blood in the holy place of Heaven, blood that is accepted by the Father once for all, and ongoing bloodshed to vindicate murderous sinners, bloodshed that never seems to be *quite* enough. This is why every generation seems to generate its own expiatory wars.

In the death of Jesus, we have the death of death. In the sacrifice of Jesus, we have the last sacrifice. In the sacrifice of Jesus, we have the death of *sacrificing*. And because Hitchens turns away from this, he is turning from the only thing that will ever be able to deal with the lunatic bloodletting which so appalls him. Hitchens objects to what he calls "propitiatory murder" (208), but in this objection he is unwittingly helping to perpetuate it.

"Once again we have a father demonstrating love by subjecting a son to death by torture, but this time the father is not trying to impress god. He *is* god, and he is trying to impress humans" (209).

On the contrary, He is not *trying* to do anything. In the death of Jesus, God was reconciling the world to Himself. Therefore the appeal to Christopher Hitchens needs to be—"be therefore reconciled." God has *done* it. Come therefore to what He has done. And what He did was not to impress humans, but to redeem them. Nothing was sufficient to deal with our corporate guilt short of the execution of the human race. This happened in the death of Jesus, the last Adam. Adam died so that the human race could die, and we died in him. Adam rose from the dead on the third day, and we were enabled to rise in Him, in order that we might walk in newness of life.

But Hitchens still objects.

> For a start, and in order to gain the benefit of this wondrous offer, I have to accept that I am responsible for the flogging and mocking and crucifixion, in which I had no say and no part . . . . Furthermore, I am required to believe that the agony was necessary in order to compensate for an earlier crime in which I also had no part, the sin of Adam. (209)

But it is simply not true that Christopher Hitchens and Douglas Wilson had no part in the rebellion of Adam. This is where Hitchens's unquestioned faith in modernity comes to the fore. He is an individualist, and he has an unquestioned philosophical commitment that requires him to think of individuals as so many marbles in a box. But we are more like individual leaves on a tree—distinct from one another, yet still connected, *always* connected. A word used by Rene Girard comes to mind—we are *interdividuals*. As leaves on a tree, we all partake of the Adamic rebellion at the root. We behave the way we do because we are sons and daughters of Adam—and not, as Hitchens is fond of saying, because we are mammals.

"We cannot, like fear-ridden peasants of antiquity, hope to load all our crimes onto a goat and then drive the hapless animal into the desert" (211). Correct. A goat won't do. What Hitchens misses is that the ancients who lived by faith were not fear-ridden peasants, as he represents them. They knew that the blood of bulls and goats was insufficient in itself. They knew that the scapegoat was not carrying anything out into the wilderness. Sacrifices and burnt offerings God did not require, but a humble and contrite heart. To obey was better than sacrifice. God desired mercy, and not sacrifice. The ancients knew this. They knew, like Abraham, that they were merely using a ritual to point to the day when the ultimate, final, and complete sacrifice would be made. And on *that* glorious day, all the sacrificial fires in all the temples of man were in principle extinguished. And God told His apostles and ministers to go out and proclaim this blessed news to the entire world. The annual tributes of blood were *over*. The propitiation was *complete*. The sacrifice was *accepted*. The smell of physical blood in worship is *done* and done forever. But it is only done in the gospel, the declaration of Christ and Him crucified.

"But I cannot absolve you of your responsibilities. It would be immoral of me to offer, and immoral of you to accept" (211). Leave aside for the moment the fact that an atheist has no basis for declaring *anything* immoral. And also leave aside the fact that he is correct that not one of us can absolve anyone else. Only God can forgive sins. But He does it in this way—so as to be just *and* the one who justifies.

God does not wave a compromise-wand over us and declare us to be forgiven. That would justify us, but He would not be just. Nor does He send us all to

Hell—then He would be just, but not the one who justifies. Rather, He sent a new Adam. He established the
whole human race all over again—Jesus Christ established a new way of being human. But the only way to
get out of the old human race and into the new one is
by means of death and resurrection. This is why there
is no injustice in the gospel. I do not simply walk away
from my sins. Sinners are guilty, and all sinners must
die. What the cross does is provide us with a way of
dying with resurrection as a promised consequence.
Jesus did not die so that we might live. *He died so that
we might die; He lives so that we might live.* This is our
hope, and this is our glory. And God in His kindness
has authorized His people to extend this offer—full of
grace—to people like Christopher Hitchens.

CHAPTER 14

HITCHENS GIVES ORWELL
THE RASPBERRY

M y review of Chapter Sixteen of Hitchens's book will not be long at all. The title of this chapter is "Is Religion Child Abuse?" He acknowledges at the conclusion of the previous chapter that it is "one provocative question" (215). It certainly is.

One of the guiding assumptions of Hitchens's zeal is that religion gets into everything and poisons it. He says that he is willing to leave the religious alone, and only wishes that they would reciprocate.

> I would not prohibit it even if I thought I could. Very generous of me, you may say. But will the religious

grant me the same indulgence? I would be quite content to go to their children's bar mitzvahs, to marvel
at their Gothic cathedrals, to "respect" their belief
that the Koran was dictated, though exclusively in
Arabic, to an illiterate merchant, or to interest myself
in Wicca and Hindu and Jain consolations. And as it
happens, I will continue to do this without insisting
on the polite reciprocal condition—which is *that they
in turn leave me alone*. But this, religion is ultimately
incapable of doing. (13, emphasis his)

Then later in the book (this chapter), he does the
same thing that Richard Dawkins did in his book *The
God Delusion*. He defines the provision of a religious
upbringing as "child abuse." Now, whenever you have
true child abuse, there is a societal duty to rescue the
child, to get that child out of the abusive home. To
make this particular point about devout homes is not
just provocative—it is inflammatory.

In this context, Hitchens puts infant baptism, the
learning of a catechism, the practice of confirmation,
Sunday School lessons, and family worship into the
same category that we use to describe the making of
child pornography, starvation, locking up in closets,
blacking eyes, and breaking bones. "What is your only
comfort in life and in death?" is, for Hitchens, in the
same category as "Who told you that you had looks or
brains, you little weasel?"

Apart from revealing that Hitchens has no sense of
proportion, and no idea of the nature of (or possibility

of) a loving Christian home, it puts the lie to his assertion that all he wants is to be left alone. In modern states, the authorities have the power to remove children from their homes if they are being abused. This is right and proper—provided they really *are* being abused. Hitchens (*and* Dawkins) are attempting to classify religious education this way, and it is a clear attempt to set the stage for the day when all children are wards of the state, *de facto* secularists. And the reason they were taken away is because their parents were not leaving *them* alone.

Of course, there would be no prohibition against parents teaching children the tenets of *Hitchens's* beliefs, for *those* beliefs are quite enlightened.

To this, my only response would be that for secularists to come for my children or grandchildren because they were being brought up in the nurture and admonition of the Lord would be right at the top of my list of horrifying examples of *not* being left alone. At our weekly sabbath dinners, I ask my grandchildren if they are baptized. Yes. I ask them if they love God. *Yes.* I ask them if Jesus is in their heart. *Yes.* I ask them if they are going to partake of the Lord's Supper in worship in the morning. *Yes.* They are short but genuine Christians. When Hitchens proposes that this should be categorized as child abuse (and we have *laws* against child abuse, do we not?), he is manifesting the totalitarian impulse that he so castigates in the next chapter.

All parents are equal when it comes to teaching their children about the world. It is just that, according to Hitchens, some parents are more equal than others. Hitchens has written a book on why Orwell matters. He should write another one on how Orwell matters more when he is understood.

CHAPTER 15

FLOATING INDIGNATION

I n Chapter Seventeen, Hitchens tries to answer the question created by secularist atrocities. A defense of God over the existence of evil is called a theodicy. A defense of atheism in light of the outrages perpetrated by secularist regimes should be called an *atheodicy*, and Hitchens offers one here. "Is it not true that secular and atheist regimes have committed crimes and massacres that are, in the scale of things, at least as bad if not worse?" (229).

There are two responses here. The first is a brief reply to Hitchens's explanation of how atheist regimes get that way. The second is a return my favorite equine carcass in order to flog it one more time.

The explanation that Hitchens puts forward for the misbehavior of atheist regimes is that when they become totalitarian, they have at that point become religions. Quoting Orwell, he says, *"A totalitarian state is in effect a theocracy,* and its ruling caste, in ordei to keep its position, has to be thought of as infallible" (232, emphasis in the original). And a bit later, Hitchens says this: "In the Bolshevik ranks, as among the Jacobins of 1789, there were also those who saw the revolution as a sort of alternative religion" (244). And this: "Communist absolutists did not so much negate religion, in societies that they well understood were saturated with faith and superstition, as seek to *replace* it (246).

All of this is insightful and dead on. But what Hitchens misses is that it is not something that the Jacobins or Marxists decided to *do.* It is inescapable. They were not in a position to *not* do it. All law is the imposition of morality, and all law systems are codified moral systems. At the head of each codified moral system is the god of the system. When you have found the source of law, you have found the god of the system. This was the case in Mosaic Israel, in Confucian China, in Marxist Russia, and in secularist Manhattan. It would be the case for any societal blueprints drafted entirely by Christopher Hitchens. *The systems differ because the gods differ.*

But Hitchens has a worldview which is entirely invisible to him. He sees that other people believe what they do and build their law orders accordingly, but when *he* proposes a law order, it is suspended in midair, based on nothing other than what "everybody knows." But everybody doesn't know it, and so the system must be modified to what "everybody who matters knows." All cultures are the incarnational outworking of a religion or combination of religions. Denying a transcendent God does not eliminate the need for a god at the top to make the system coherent. It just means that the applicants for the position of deity are all, to use one of Hitchens's favorite words, mammals. It can be just one mammal, as in North Korea, or it can be fifty million mammals with a system of primary elections, a general election, and topped off with an electoral college election. If there is no God above the system, then the system *is* god. All societies are religious organisms, not just the ones with a religious exoskeleton.

This is nothing other than to call Orwell and raise him ten. All human societies are theocracies. The only issue that confronts us is which *theos* we will serve. The atrocious cultures are the ones who serve atrocious gods. And if an atrocious one does what it does in the name of the Father of the Lord Jesus Christ (and Hitchens has numerous examples of *that* in this chapter), then this reveals the true god of the system. Devil worship is not cleaned up or transformed by doing it all in the name of Jesus. The devil *loves* doing things in the name of Jesus.

This brings us back to my dead horse. By what standard? I am afraid that Hitchens has missed the central ethical problem that atheism faces, and he has missed that point again.

> Humanism has many crimes for which to apologize. But it can apologize for them, and also correct them, in its own terms and without having to shake or challenge the basis of any unalterable system of belief. (250)

This is mere hand-waving. What *are* "its own terms"? And humanism is supposed to have an advantage over traditional religion (the ones with an unalterable system of belief) because it can apologize for "crimes" without having to bring any challenge to an unalterable system of belief. You see, the gods in heaven don't change their minds, so when traditional religion is confronted with various crimes, the challenge goes right down to their foundations. Well, in the case of many traditional religions, the challenge *needs* to go right down to the foundations. Again, the Christian is identified, not with religion generally, but with Christ specifically.

But that is not our concern here. Our concern right now is humanism. Humanism can apologize for its crimes because it doesn't have an unalterable foundation, and it is therefore *flexible*. Humanism is not all stiff in the joints like some other hidebound traditions we could name. But if humanism doesn't have an unalterable foundation, then its foundation must be alterable. And if its foundation is alterable, one of the things that can be altered is the definition of *what constitutes a crime in the first place.*

It amazes me that someone of Hitchens's intelligence does not see this. As I have noted before, Hitchens is a gifted writer. This means he has a boatload of vivid adjectives and nouns at his fingertips. But, also as noted before, a boatload of vivid adjectives and nouns *does not make up a coherent moral system.* Hitchens can say, and indeed does say, things like *megalomania, bovine elders, vile, ravings, deranged, piffle, hideous din, pathetic mammal son,* and *arrogant* and *insufferable belief.* But why does any of that matter?

Hitchens acknowledges *that* secularist hellholes are wrong. He explains (in many ways, accurately) *how* they came to be so wrong. In many cases it was because of the previous misbehavior of believers. Granted. He vividly lances the pomposity and pretensions of those who are wrong in this way. The only thing he does not explain—*for he cannot explain it*—is *why* they are wrong.

But we know from this chapter that his indignation is not grounded on the bedrock of anything that is "unalterable." His indignation is therefore a floating indignation. It is not anchored. It is not grounded. It is not fixed. And like all such things that float on the surface of turbulent ocean currents, in a couple generations that indignation is likely to be a long way away from *here.*

CHAPTER 16

THE TOP HAT AND THE SEA OTTERS

We are in the backstretch now. In his next chapter, Christopher Hitchens gives us a brief historical survey of freethinkers throughout history who found themselves in trouble with the authorities. Men like Socrates, Spinoza, and Thomas Paine are an inspiration to Hitchens, and he spends this chapter telling us why. But he also tells us some other things in the course of his discussion, revealing a good deal more than he can afford to reveal.

He says that one of the things we learn from Socrates—and it is of "highest importance"—is the fact that "conscience is innate" (256). Well, fine, if he wants to locate it like that. But what we really need to know is whether conscience is *authoritative*. My ability to hiccup is innate, but my hiccups are not authoritative. We need more than a bare assertion. On what basis do we say that my own conscience is a moral arbiter, even with regard to my *own* affairs? And taking it up to the next level of difficulty, how does an individualist like Hitchens possibly get to a "societal conscience"?

Right at the center of my conscience is the duty I know I have to render thanksgiving and gratitude to God. Is this requirement of my conscience binding on Hitchens? He would say *no*, but then he would have to say that this is because such a duty is not *really* part of the innate conscience that everybody has. But who is Hitchens to come prying around in my conscience like that? In what way is his conscience authoritative over mine?

Hitchens believes (and just asserts) that the dictates of conscience which must be followed are those which require us to pay attention to "mutual interest and solidarity."

> In this summary of mutual interest and solidarity, there is no requirement for any enforcing or supernatural authority. And why should there be? Human decency is not derived from religion. It precedes it. (266)

A host of questions arise at this point. If human decency is not derived from religion, but rather precedes it, what would Hitchens think of the statement that religion was therefore derived from human decency? Well, he wouldn't like that, because he believes that religion poisons everything. But note where this leaves him. Mankind, basically good, basically decent, cooked up the mechanisms of religion, the reeking altars of which darken the sun and blacken the sky. And this means that Hitchens, as much as he does not want to, has to give an account of human *indecency*.

So let's give it to him. Human decency is not derived from religion but precedes it. Human indecency is not derived from religion either but precedes it. Human decency and human indecency both proceed from the human heart. Now how do we decide between them? Decency might have some evolutionary advantages for your tribe, so long as it is carefully restricted to your own tribe. But spread that decency around too much you might only succeed in getting your little portion of the gene pool wiped out.

So we don't have religion yet. All we have are certain impulses to what later ages will call the convention of decency along with other impulses that they will call indecency. The only basis we have for deciding between them is the overriding impulse directed at the survival of my own DNA. Sounds like what is needed around here is to rape all the female captives.

When Hitchens appeals to things like innate conscience and human decency, doing so as an evolutionary atheist, he is functioning as an illusionist. What

218 GOD IS: HOW CHRISTIANITY EXPLAINS EVERYTHING

he is doing is *transparently* a trick. Even if a Christian reader doesn't know how he is doing that trick, it is manifestly a trick that he is doing. And it is a pretty good one, too. He did not pull a rabbit out of a hat—he pulled three sea otters out of that thing. The sea otters are now lined up on the stage, and we can make out their embossed names on the collars—human decency, innate conscience, and solidarity. But regardless of what you think you have seen, the battered top hat of atheism does not really produce sea otters. Unless you give it ten million years. *Then* it is a possibility I guess.

And last, Hitchens quotes Epicurus, in his statement of the age-old problem of evil. "Is he willing to prevent evil but not able? Then he is impotent. Is he able but not willing? Then he is malevolent. Is he both able and willing? Whence then is evil?" (268).

This is a very good statement of the problem. But then Hitchens adds that atheism "cuts through this non-quandary like the razor of Ockham" (268). Right. But it only cuts through the "non-quandary" by postulating a universe in which all evil has to be understood as "non-evil." And Hitchens does this right at the conclusion of a book filled with more expressions of indignant, puritanical outrage than I have read in a long time. "There is no such thing as evil, and those who argue with me on this point are wicked, stupid, or both."

Hitchens doesn't cut through the problem of evil with Ockham's razor. He takes the granite hard problem of evil and daubs at it with Ockham's pound of wet liver.

CHAPTER 17

DESCRIPTION AND EXPLANATION

C hristopher Hitchens concludes his book, and I conclude my review of it, with Chapter Nineteen: "In Conclusion: The Need for a New Enlightenment." But if this is enlightenment, we need to check the batteries.

"Religion has run out of justifications. Thanks to the telescope and the microscope, it no longer offers an explanation of anything important" (282).

It seems fitting to end this series of reviews with a short parable.

A certain man of the eighteenth century was speaking with an infidel, one who had spent much time in the salons of Paris. He did this because it was the best place to meet sophist chicks. When the infidel found out that the other man was a believer in God, he put his head back and he scoffed. After a moment, he scoffed *again*, directly at the sky. The other man offered the infidel a lozenge.

"What's that?" the infidel wanted to know. "It's a scoff suppressant," the believer said.

"It'll take more than *that*, my friend," said the infidel.

"Why do you say this?" said the believer.

"Perhaps you are unaware of the engines of knowledge that modern men have been able to build?"

"Perhaps I am, depending on what you mean by *knowledge*."

"I refer, of course, to the microscope and the telescope. Your religious beliefs offered us comfortable explanations *once*, but that was before we invented these most excellent devices."

"You mean to say that if you look at something closely enough, all need for explanation vanishes?"

"What?"

"Look, let me be the infidel for a moment. You be the Christian."

"All right."

"Do you see that tree over there? The one about twenty yards away?"

"I do."

"Let us walk half the distance toward the tree."

A moment passed, and there was only the sound of crunching gravel.

"Now, can you make the tree out more clearly? The outlines of the bark? The roots as they slope down to the grass?"

"Yes, I see it much more distinctly. I can even count the leaves."

"So where's your God *now*, friend?"

Christopher Hitchens does not know the difference between *greater detail of description* and *explanation*. If he would like a further explanation of this point, I would suggest that he double the font size of this chapter and read it again. And if greater clarity of vision is tantamount to explanation, *everything* should become perfectly clear.

THE DELUDED ATHEIST

A RESPONSE
TO RICHARD DAWKINS'S *THE GOD DELUSION*

.

CHAPTER 1

LET'S FRITZ OUR BRAINS
AT THEM

R ichard Dawkins wants to raise our consciousness—to "raise consciousness to the fact that
to be an atheist is a realistic aspiration, and
a brave and splendid one" (1).[1] And his 2006 book,
The God Delusion, certainly does have some high aspira-
tions in this regard. As high, that is, as approximate-
ly one hundred and eighty pounds of protoplasm can
have. Get yourself a double-layered Hefty garbage bag
and fill it with some kind of vegetable soup, shake it

---

1. Throughout this book, the page numbers given in parentheses refer to Richard Dawkins, *The God Delusion* (New York: Houghton Mifflin, 2008).

for a bit, and you have some idea of just how lofty an aspiration can actually be.

But the point is apparently not how high the aspiration has to *be*, but what you can get other bits of protoplasm to say about it in the blurbs, which is almost as good. But they need to say it in an energetic enough way to sway the general mass of protoplasmic bipedal carbon units out there, which is to say, the reading public. Because if enough bits of protoplasm get together on this, we can get ourselves a consensus going, and first thing you know you are dealing with the voice of Reason. The voice of Reason is what happens when any kind of physical wave (sound waves are best) shudders through a portion of the vegetable soup, dispelling the voice of Superstition forever.

Still, the blurbs are kinda fun. The noted intellectuals Penn and Teller say this: "*The God Delusion* is smart, compassionate, and true like ice, like fire. If this book doesn't change the world, we're all screwed."

Ahhhhuuhh. True like ice. True like fire. But how true are *those*? How true are they together? Does the fire melt the ice, or does the melted ice put out the fire? Or both perhaps? True like a puddle with charcoal in it? Now we're talking.

And then Philip Pullman, author of the *His Dark Materials* trilogy, said this, while obviously holding back: "Many religious leaders today are men who, it's obvious to anyone but their deranged followers, are willing to sanction vicious cruelty in the service of their faith. Dawkins hits them with all the power that reason can wield."

Let me go on record right *now* as saying that vicious cruelty is bad, and maybe it is here that we atheists and Christians can actually find some common ground and move the discussion forward but, come to think of it, probably not.

Now of course, it's kind of early in my response to be pointing this out, but the thing has to be done some time. If that is the case, then why not make the point every other page or so? Or at least until someone gets it enough to attempt an answer. Reason, being a quaint and superstitious name we give to random neuron firings in the brain, *wields no power at all.* On atheistic principles, expecting to find a correlation called "truth" between the chemical activities of the cerebral cortex in *some* people and the outside world is more than a little bit like astrology—or tying the bulls and bears of the stock market to the batting averages of professional baseball players. Can be done, I suppose, but why would we ever think that *this* random dance of atoms had anything whatever to do with *that* random dance of atoms?

"Fearless atheist leader, look! There goes a *religious* leader, with his deranged minions behind him! They are going out to perpetrate another vicious cruelty and will perhaps even differ with us! Whatever shall we do?"

"Don't waver, Bertrand. We shall wield the force of Reason. All together now—let's fritz our brains at them!" We are only in the preface to the book, but Dawkins begins with the idea that we religious types need to lay off the kids. He wants us to get jumpy about expressing ourselves too freely about that "nurture and admonition of the Lord" stuff. "That is not a Muslim child, but a child of Muslim parents. That child is too young to know whether it is a Muslim or not. There is no such thing as a Muslim child. There is no such thing as a Christian child" (3).

And of course, arid cognition is king around here. That child is also too young to know if it is a boy or a girl, and it therefore follows that it must be neither. That child is too young to know if it is Canadian or Swiss, so it must belong to a holding tank at the United Nations. Apparently, Dawkins instinctively felt that he was losing me with his deep argumentation right around this point, so he presses on to explain how it was that I got so silly.

> If this book works as I intend, religious readers will be atheists when they put it down. What presumptuous optimism! Of course, dyed-in-the-wool faith-heads are immune to argument, their resistance built up over years of childhood indoctrination using methods that took centuries to mature (whether by evolution or design). Among the more effective immunological devices is a dire warning to avoid even

opening a book like this, which is surely a work of Satan. (5–6)

I don't know. I would more inclined to consider it a jesuitical work of the Holy Spirit, designed to make lapsed Christians, who had unreflectingly drifted into a secular mindset, go running back to the Church in a panic.

That's us! Immune to argument! They bounce right off *my* forehead, but even so, we Christians have to pretend to argue sometimes, to keep up appearances. Let's see how it goes.

CHAPTER 2

PSALTER, CLAYMORE, AND BAGPIPES

The first chapter of *The God Delusion* is divided into two sections. The first section is entitled "Deserved Respect," and talks about scientists like Einstein, Hawking, and others who use religious terminology to talk about the whoa factor when it comes to just how cool the universe actually is. It is beyond dispute that lots of people (including scientists) get overwhelmed by the majesty of everything, and this regularly evokes religiouslike sentiments, and that sometimes leads to religiouslike forms of expression, even from the scientists. If traditional believers hear this language, they can too often jump to conclusions, and enlist the scientist in question on the side of the angels. Not so fast, says Dawkins. There is not really a lot to talk about here—I quite agree that Einstein did not believe in a personal god. I think Dawkins does a decent job—the only substantive difference I would have with him is that he says that this is the only kind of religious expression that is deserving of respect. But of course that one difference makes all the difference.

"As I continue to clarify the distinction between supernatural religion on the one hand and Einsteinian religion on the other, bear in mind that I am calling only *supernatural* gods delusional" (15). Well, I too think lots of gods are delusional. Especially Thor. But we ought not to get distracted by these peripheral issues. We have other fish, as they say, to fry.

The second part of this chapter begins Dawkins's treatment of those expressions of religion that are *not* deserving of respect, and he certainly does not intend to render it. Quoting Mencken, he says that he will respect the other fellow's religion, "but only in the sense and to the extent that we respect his theory that his wife is beautiful and his children smart" (27).

> The metaphorical or pantheistic God of the physicists is light years away from the interventionist, miracle-wreaking, thought-reading, sin-punishing, prayer-answering God of the Bible, of priests, mullahs and rabbis, and of ordinary language. (19)

Dawkins thinks that "religions" of this latter type are way too pampered in our society, and that it has gotten to the point where no one is allowed to criticize something that is plainly nuts, provided that said something is done in the name of some religion or other. Ordinary activities and pursuits are not pampered in the same way. And he really has a point here, up to a point. Speaking of a court case where a religious group was allowed to use drugs for the sake of their "religion," he says,

> Religion, as ever, is the trump card. Imagine members of an art appreciation society pleading in court that they 'believe' they need a hallucinogenic drug in order to enhance their understanding of Impressionist or Surrealist paintings. (22)

Now I don't want to go down a rabbit trail here, but it seems to me that a case arguing the need for hallucinogenic drugs in order to appreciate much that goes on in the contemporary art world could be quite a compelling one—but to pursue this point would take us too far afield. I want to get to the basic structural problem with how Dawkins is setting up the argument for the book.

He is quite right that many crazy things are done in the name of religion. He is also right that many crazy things are done in the name of the *Christian* religion. And so, in a deft move worthy of a young Napoleon in the field, he sets every form of supernatural religion on the one side (where they must all stand or fall together), and naturalism on the other. He sets this up as the choice before us, and he is now in a position to roll up his sleeves, spit on his hands, and get to work. But wait a minute. Let's do the same thing on another subject entirely. The content of the debate will change, but the structure of argumentation will be identical to that being used by Dawkins here. Instead of supernaturalism v. naturalism, let's make it "medical treatments" v. "no medical treatments."

The man who believes in "no medical treatments" can (if he remains healthy long enough) become quite a scourge for those bozos who believe in "medical treatments." Every time the issue comes up, the skeptic can glibly refer to snake oil, naturopathy, eye of newt, chemotherapy, high fiber diets, chelation therapy, crystal healings, and antibiotics. These are all varied species of the genus "medical treatments." And, you know, they *are*. The way this argument is constructed, the most sane medical doctor in the world has to answer for the juju bean cancer treatments, sold for a buck fifty at your nearby All Natural Health Emporium.

If the sane doctor tries to protest that he is against all the craziness in the "medical treatments" world, the skeptic has structured things in such a way that makes it most easy to disbelieve him.

"I refuse to believe you until you sever all ties with your fellow believers."

"I am not a fellow believer. I don't believe in the juju beans *at all*."

"You say that, but you continue to administer your own medications, do you not?"

"Well, yes . . ."

"Which also come in bottles? With printed labels?"

When Dawkins lights into radical Muslims going crazy over the Danish cartoons, I am right with him. Something really needs to be done about those people. When he talks about how Pope John Paul II made *way* too many people saints, my Scottish covenanter blood begins to rise, and I start hunting around for the psalter, claymore, and bagpipes. I begin muttering *aye* to myself.

But then I come back to earth. And I wonder, how is it that a false medical treatment can be used as an argument against all medical treatments? How does that work? How do forgeries prove that there is no original? How do counterfeiters show that there is no such thing as real money? Ah, I think to myself. There is some kind of funny business going on here.

CHAPTER 3

A COUPLE OF JUNIOR HIGH GIRLS IN A SLAP FIGHT

D awkins spends a goodish bit of time in his first chapter trying to show that belief in supernatural religion is not worthy of the thinking man's respect.

> It is in the light of the unparalleled presumption of respect for religion that I make my own disclaimer for this book. I shall not go out of my way to offend, but nor shall I don kid gloves to handle religion any more gently than I would handle anything else (27)

That is right at the end of chapter one. Having thus prepared us, the first words in chapter two are these:

The God of the Old Testament is arguably the most
unpleasant character in all fiction: jealous and proud
of it; a petty, unjust, unforgiving control-freak; a vin-
dictive, bloodthirsty ethnic cleanser; a misogynistic,
homophobic, racist, infanticidal, genocidal, filicidal,
pestilential, megalomaniacal, sadomasochistic, capri-
ciously malevolent bully. (31)

Well, Richard, don't hold back on our account. Now
let us spend a few moments addressing the ethics of
polemical exchange. This topic usually gravitates toward the question of what kind of thing is "above the
belt" and what is "below the belt." This is an important question, worthy of consideration in its own right,
but there is a related question I want to address here
because it is an obvious factor in the rise of the "new
atheism." More than one observer has noted that there
has been a new wave of atheistic writers who belong
to the "take no prisoners" school of thought. Previous
atheists had adopted the strategy of an urbane sophis-
tication, an attitude that rose above the unwashed superstitions of the masses. We theists were allowed our
silly beliefs and practices, and "educated people" had
the confidence to know that these assumptions of ours
presented no threat whatever to the continued regency
of unbelief. After all, we were offering up our ineffec-
tual prayers to that great nullity in the sky from red
state flyover country, and the real action was occurring
in the corridors of cultural power in New York, L.A.,
and Washington, D.C.

This patronizing attitude on the part of atheists appears to be disappearing, and there are deep reasons for it. I speak as a conservative Christian who has felt (for thirty years or more) that the besetting sin of Christian conservatives was the sin of conducting polemical warfare with the really bad motive mix of hatred, panic, and fear. The end result was a hard-hitting polemic that was invariably *shrill*. In contrast, I have sought, over many years, to cultivate a manner of polemical exchange that is willing to hit hard but from a position of strength and confidence, or, to speak in biblical categories, from a position of faith. It is not enough to be in the "right," and it is not enough to be striking the "right" person. That can happen when two junior high girls get in a slap fight over a boy with acne.

What has happened to the atheists and unbelievers is this: they have begun to see their hegemonic control over public discourse begin to slip away. Educated people are starting to question, in *public*, some of the sacred objects that had been safely sealed up in their secular *sanctum sanctorum*. Confronted with this, they have responded as badly as some Christians did when the same thing started to happen to us several centuries ago. In other words, I know what this kind of shrillness smells like. We have been guilty of it in far too many ways. But now the fundamentalist secularists, men like Dawkins and Harris, are starting to behave in just the way that fundamentalists do. When everything you hold dear appears to be threatened, one of the easiest things to do is to drift into a no-holds-barred mindset. Some Christians, reacting to panicked flame-throwing of fearful Christians, have opted for the opposite error. Tepid, balanced, irenic, and boring, they follow in the steps of the Master as He was conceived by effeminate painters of the Victorian era—*that* Jesus could have done advertisements for Clairol. For such Christians, any kind of fight at all is a bad testimony.

All this to say that I, like Dawkins, am not going to go out of my way to offend. But, unlike Dawkins, I have no intention of letting this sign of panic among the Philistines lure me into any kind of polemical imitation. I want to fight like D'Artagnan and not like Tiffany.

CHAPTER 4

THE GUY IN THE TEAPOT

N ot surprisingly, Richard Dawkins places the evolutionary process at the center of his argument. "This book will advocate an alternative view: *any creative intelligence, of sufficient complexity to design anything, comes into existence only as the end product of an extended process of gradual evolution*" (31, emphasis in the original).

This might be hard for scientific laymen to grasp, so I will try to provide a couple of illustrations. This factory, for example, full of fantastically complex machinery and robots for the manufacturing of various ingenious devices of intricate design, is something that cannot itself be designed. For when confronted with a world full of designed things, it is *not* unscientific to allow that many of them were in fact designed, so long as you insist that the most intricate and complicated one, the one making all the others, happened all by itself. This Swiss watch exhibits design, to be sure, and we can allow that it was made, on purpose, in the factory. But the factory for making Swiss watches, far more complicated than any of the watches made in said factory, had to have been the result of a huge explosion in a nearby auto salvage yard. If you don't follow this argument, you probably didn't take enough science courses in high school.

If you need to hang some really heavy things from your sky hook, make sure to fasten the socket for that sky hook at least fifteen feet higher in the air than you otherwise would. The bolts work better a little bit higher like that.

Before I get some comments from scientists who think that I am not being sufficiently respectful, let me defend myself by quoting Dawkins quoting Thomas Jefferson:

> Ridicule is the only weapon which can be used against unintelligible propositions. Ideas must be distinct before reason can act upon them; and no man ever had a distinct idea of the trinity. It is the mere Abracadabra of the mountebanks calling themselves the priests of Jesus. (34)

I am glad that Dawkins taught me this principle, for I have long failed to comprehend any *distinct* notion of something that travels like a wave and arrives like a particle. Or maybe it is the other way around, traveling like a particle and arriving like a wave. See? A positively *indistinct* concept. I don't think it could be me.

The backdrop for many of Dawkins's worries is his idea that the United States has turned into this huge theocracy. And, by European standards, maybe we have, but that is not saying much.

> The paradox has often been noted that the United States, founded in secularism, is now the most religiose country in Christendom, while England, with an established church headed by its constitutional monarch, is among the least. (40)

Dawkins swallows the standard propaganda about the deism of the Founders and laments how far our fair republic has fallen. "The genie of religious fanaticism is rampant in present-day America, and the Founding Fathers would have been horrified" (41).

Horrified, aye. The preachers at the time of the American founding were the kind of men who spit on their hands before they started to preach, and, taking one thing with another, they made the average religious right evangelical *today* look like the Rev. Caspar Milquetoast. At Yorktown, all but one of George Washington's colonels were elders in Presbyterian churches. Horace Walpole said, "Cousin America has run off with a

Presbyterian parson," referring to Witherspoon. Over half of the Continental Army were Presbyterians, and the rest were Congregationalists and Baptists, fellow Calvinists all. The blackrobed Presbyterian preachers were called "the black regiment" because of their importance to the war effort. In England, one of the nicknames for the war was "the Presbyterian Revolt." I could go on, but Richard Dawkins seriously needs to strike up a friendship with Gary DeMar and try to sneevle some free books out of him.

All that may be, but luckily it doesn't matter.

> Whether Jefferson and his colleagues were theists, deists, agnostics or atheists, they were also passionate secularists who believed that the religious opinions of a President, or lack of them, were entirely his own business. (43)

Here is Jefferson's famous wall of separation, the wall that separates, as every intelligent school child knows, the right side of the brain from the left side of the brain. This wall, so important in modern secular politics, prevents us from thinking straight, for, as we all know, thinking straight would lead us into Difficulties.

I am fond of the following thought experiment. A man is running for high office, and in the course of the campaign he says this, in response to a question: "You know, my faith is very precious to me—too precious in fact to mix with the secular duties that are connected with this office. If elected, I pledge to the American people that I will *not* allow my private religious convictions to affect in any way how I discharge my duties." Two years later when he is found with two hundred thousand dollars in his freezer, a mistress in the Bahamas, Jack Abramoff in his closet, and dry rot in his soul, certain penetrating questions are asked at a press conference. But the best defense is a good offense, and I would love to see Sen. Snoutworst stick to his guns. "There is *nothing* to apologize for in this. I openly promised the American people in the campaign that my personal religious convictions, which are very precious to Cathy and me (not to mention Kimberly), would not be allowed to intrude into how I conducted myself in office." Secularism defined this way is not just wrong, it is incoherent.

But this is a book about atheism, and so we get back to the God issue. Dawkins brings forth Bertrand Russell's argument concerning the burden of proof. If someone were to assert that between Earth and Mars a china teapot was orbiting the sun elliptically (52) and that it was too small to be detected by our most powerful telescopes, it would be impossible to prove the theory wrong. But Russell argued that the burden of proof remains on the teapot enthusiast. Okay, I can go for that. So why is this a bad example on the God question? Why are the outer space teapot and the God who created all things not comparable? The reason they don't compare is that God *does* things, and He *says* things. If the teapot were out there *and sending messages*, we would know how to decode those messages. Dawkins actually acknowledges this in his discussion (in this same chapter) of the search for extraterrestrial intelligence. While talking about our attempts to understand messages coming toward us, he asks, "A good approach is to turn the question around. What should we intelligently do in order to advertise our presence to extraterrestrial listeners?" (71).

Very good. And if someone in this cosmic teapot were sending SOS messages because the cosmic tea cozy got stuck and he could not get away in the standard teapot escape pod (as the apostle Paul would put it, I am out of my mind to talk like this), we would know how to decode his distress messages because we have the ability to distinguish information from background noise. *We know what information looks like.* Now, what if the universe we live in has information embedded in it throughout? What if the triune God who spoke it all into existence has left notes everywhere? What if every living cell contains a library that makes the Library of Congress look like my grandkids' coloring book collection?

Dawkins gets one thing right:

> As I shall argue in a moment, a universe with a creative superintendent would be a very different kind

of universe from one without. Why is that not a scientific matter? (55)

I return to the point: a universe in which we are alone
except for other slowly evolved intelligences is a very
different universe from one with an original guiding
agent whose intelligent design is responsible for its
very existence. (61)

He is quite right. A universe spoken into existence
by God is a very different place than a chaotic mul-
tiverse that has just staggered onto the cosmic stage
and is looking around bewildered. "What *is* this?" it
whispers frantically. "Waiting for Godot" the prompter
hisses back.

"Like nothing else, evolution really does provide
an explanation for the existence of entities whose
improbability would otherwise, for practical purposes, rule them out" (61). Right. Libraries write themselves, factories build themselves, and bridges design
themselves. This doesn't usually happen, to be sure,
and if it weren't for *evolution*, it would be reasonable
for us to rule such things out. In fact, I think the only
person who wouldn't rule them out would be the guy
in the teapot.

CHAPTER 5

THE CRAWL SPACE UNDER THE NEUTRAL ZONE

The next chapter of Dawkins's book concerns the arguments for God's existence. He addresses, in turn, the traditional Thomist arguments, the ontological argument, the aesthetic argument, the argument from personal experience, the argument from Scripture, the argument from admired religious scientists, Pascal's wager, and a Bayesian argument involving probability calculations.

Not surprisingly, since Dawkins is an atheist, he finds none of these arguments compelling. But it is not enough to flip it around and assume that a Christian would have to find them all compelling. Some of them are quite bad, and all of them are misplaced.

The problem is the setup. If we assume some sort of neutral zone in which we do not know whether God exists or not, and then we set ourselves the task of reasoning our way out of this zone into some kind of conclusion for or against, we have already conceded something that no consistent Christian should grant. We have conceded that it is theoretically possible for us to be here and God not to be here. This is not just false; it is incoherent. More on this in a moment.

Given the fact of the living God, what are we to do with these arguments? Some of them fail even though their conclusion is true—using the language of the logicians, the fact that the conclusion is true doesn't make the argument valid. If I were to argue that George Washington was the first president because (and only because) I had buttered toast for breakfast this morning, I am reasoning badly. I don't help matters by giving my *non sequitur* a pious sheen by arguing that God exists because I had buttered toast this morning. Which I didn't, by the way, but work with me here. Poor arguments from the list above would include Pascal's wager, the Bayesian argument, and the argument from admired religious scientists. When Dawkins has his fun with them, who am I to deny him a bit of sunshine and jollity in his otherwise blinkered existence?

The remaining arguments are fine, but why do I say they are misplaced? I don't accept that it is legitimate for us to go into some neutral zone, put the question of God up for grabs, notice that the sunset is beautiful, and come to the conclusion that God exists. I grant that the sunset is beautiful, and it is beautiful because God exists, and if God didn't exist, it wouldn't be there to be beautiful. But God is always the foundation, the premise, never the conclusion. He is not the one we travel to; He is the one in whom we live and move and have our being. Another way of saying this is that the aesthetic argument doesn't prove God's existence, but rather the fact of the triune God establishes the aesthetic argument.

The same kind of thing with the ontological argument and the argument from design and so on. St. Paul says plainly enough in Romans that God's majesty is plainly visible in the things that have been made, but this is only because He created them and put them there. The (neutral) argument from design is simultaneously true and insolent. And because such arguments are frequently pursued by men who want a pretense of objectivity (which they can have only if the possibility of getting *either* answer is guaranteed), this puts the one presenting or listening to the argument in the position of judge. But this inverts everything. *God* is the only judge. And He says (in Scripture) that unrighteous men suppress the truth. Their knowledge of God is like a giant beach ball that they have been holding under water for their entire time in the pool, and their arms are getting all trembly.

When I knock on the door of the neutral zone, Dawkins opens the door, all smiles. Another Christian. "Sure, let's discuss it," he says. "Let's hear *your* argument for God's existence. But I have to warn you—I think I have heard just about everything."

"Oh, I don't want to argue for the existence of God," I say.

He looks surprised. "Why did you come here then?"

"I saw the sign on the door—*neutral zone*. I have always wanted to know what one of *those* might be. So I guess I am interested in hearing your arguments for the existence of a neutral zone."

"Well, this is a bit unusual, but the neutral zone is the place where we agree to reason together about ultimate questions . . . like the existence of God."

"Reason. What's that?"

"Reason is the process of identifying rational inferences from true and established premises."

"Is this *reason* authoritative? Do we have a moral obligation to obey it?"

"Well, yes."

"Why?"

"Because to do otherwise would be . . . unreasonable."

"I have questioned your Scriptures, and didn't you just defend them by pointing to a Bible verse?"

"So you are opposed to reason. Is that right?"

"Well, no. I am happy to follow reason wherever it goes. But before we follow it anywhere, we first have to know where it came from. I am interested in the preconditions of reason. You have said that reason is the rule to follow in this neutral zone. But what is this neutral zone resting on? What is the foundation? Have you ever gone down into the crawl space under this neutral zone with a flashlight? To see what it is resting on?"

"I have no idea what you are talking about."

"Well, I know that. You devoted thirty-two pages of your book to the arguments for God's existence, and you completely ignored the transcendental argument. It is as though you had never heard of it, which is inexplicable in a writer of your stature. You teach at Oxford, after all, and not at Cow Tech. You would think that you would be able to identify your own presuppositions—and what they are resting on."

"What do *you* say they rest on?"

"Well, what else? They rest on the Incarnation, death, and Resurrection of our Lord Jesus Christ. And before we reason any further about it, I really think we should ask the Lord to bless our endeavors."

"*You* are begging the question."

"I know. That's inescapable with all ultimate questions. So let's ask God to bless that too."

CHAPTER 6

CEREAL OR EGGS?

T
he next chapter is the heart of Dawkins's book, so the best plan would seem to be to take more than one installment to deal with it. At the conclusion of this chapter, Dawkins says that "this chapter has contained the central argument of my book" (157), which is actually kind of scary when you think about it. But a lot of people are listening to Dawkins, and so I don't think it will be a waste of time to go over his argument more closely in this section.

An essential component of his argument is the distinction he makes between *chance* and *natural selection*. He cheerfully grants to the creationist that complex things don't just spring into being by chance. There is nothing chancy about it, Dawkins argues. Design versus chance is a false alternative. "The argument from improbability states that complex things could not have come about by chance. But many people *define* 'come about by chance' as a synonym for 'come about in the absence of deliberate design" (114).

> Creationist 'logic' is always the same. Some natural phenomenon is too statistically improbable, too complex, too beautiful, too awe-inspiring to have come into existence by chance. Design is the only alternative to chance that the authors can imagine. Therefore a designer must have done it. And science's answer to this faulty logic is also always the same. Design is not the only alternative to chance. Natural selection is a better alternative. (121)

Dawkins admits in multiple places that the *appearances* are against him. "Who, before Darwin, could have guessed that something so apparently designed as a dragonfly's wing or an eagle's eye was really the end product of a long sequence of non-random but purely natural causes" (116).

Now look closely at this quotation. These magnificent organs (and scadzillions like them) are "really the end product of a long sequence of *non-random* but purely natural causes." Non-random? Well, he has to say that, because he is arguing that chance and natural selection are two different things. But the foundation of natural selection is mutation. How do mutations occur? Randomly or non-randomly? Ah, exactly so.

Dawkins might want to qualify his point here and grant that the *mutations* are random, dealt out of the deck by a blindfolded dealer, but then go on to say that his point really was that while the mutations are random, the *survival* of the lucky critter that received a beneficial mutation (by chance) is not random. That's not what he said, but let's allow him to qualify it. The increased odds of survival are, I grant, explicable as a non-random thing, provided something happens that actually increases a creature's ability to adapt to his environment. But we will pursue this, and the idea of irreducible complexity, in another installment.

With regard to *this* part of his argument, my critique of Dawkins is simple—Dawkins is missing the point in a spectacular way. We are having an argument over what possible options we have for breakfast—cereal or eggs? That is a false alternative Dawkins insists. Why can't we have an omelet instead? But omelets are made up of eggs, and natural selection is *made up of* a host of random, chance events. And at least the omelet has the decency to limit itself to just *three* eggs. Just one stupendous piece of engineering like the dragonfly's wing would require gazillions of *chance* mutations, most of them negative and harmful, and the rest of them entirely inadequate.

Driving through a nice neighborhood with Dawkins, we drive by a nice colonial-looking pile. "Oh, look," I say, pointing. "Brick!" "That's not brick," Dawkins replies. "That's a house. You Americans and your theocracy!"

The brazen part comes next. Dawkins instinctively *knows* that he is doing an adroit word game shuffle.

Natural selection works because it is a cumulative one-way street to improvement. It needs some luck to get started, and the 'billions of planets' anthropic principle grants it that luck. Maybe a few later gaps in the evolutionary story also need major infusions of luck, with anthropic justification. (141)

Another name for the anthropic principle is the Goldilocks principle (141ff). Conditions can't be too cold or too hot for life to arise—they have to be "just right." The earth can't be too close to the sun or too far away, and so on.

But look what Dawkins did here, right out in broad daylight. Substitute *chance* or *chance event* for *luck* in the quotation above and ask yourself if the meaning is materially altered. Well, no, not in the slightest. So the evolutionary story needs "major infusions" of *chance* the way the omelet needs "major infusions" of egg. Dawkins admits he needs luck to jump the chasm between inorganic and organic matter, and he kind of allows that he needs luck to get the origin of the eukaryotic cell (the kind we have), and the origin of consciousness "might be" another place requiring this kind of astronomical luck. But don't call it chance, you bozo, because that would be an admission that the only alternative to chance is design.

One last comment on this point. Dawkins uses a parable to describe the task of "climbing Mount Improbable." On one side is a radical cliff, and Dawkins grants that a lowly creature at the bottom of the cliff cannot suddenly leap to the top of the cliff, becoming another kind of creature instantly. That violates the laws of probability in such a way as to be functionally impossible. But on the other side of the mountain is a long gradual slope, up which, over time, creatures can evolve. It is a clever illustration. We all nod, yes, a turtle can't suddenly fly up the cliff face, and yes, a turtle could walk up a gradual slope and get to the top. Q.E.D. Not exactly. This is not illustrating the point at issue.

Let's have the turtle at the bottom of the cliff jumping, and by the time, seconds later, when he is at the top, he is now an English professor at Ball State. Okay, so improbable as to be impossible. Now take the turtle around to the gradual slope, tell him to walk up slowly, take ten million years if he wants, but he still has to be an English professor at Ball State when he gets to the top. Is this any more likely?

CHAPTER 7

A COLORLESS, ODORLESS GAS WITH LOTS OF POTENTIAL

In this centerpiece chapter, Dawkins sets out to turn the tables on the creationists, and he wants to do so in an elegant way. His argument reminds me of a comment once made to my brother-in-law (a pediatric cardiologist) by another doctor, an atheist. He said that the liver was so complicated, *God* couldn't even make one. And that settles that, right?

Anyhow, here it is. Dawkins keys off an illustration used by the great scientist Fred Hoyle, who said that the probability of life happening on earth by itself was comparable to the probability of a hurricane sweeping through a junk yard having the luck to assemble a Boeing 747. I think Hoyle might be granting them too much here, but still, I sympathize with the sentiment. Here is how Dawkins wants to turn this around. "However statistically improbable the entity you seek to explain by invoking a designer, the designer himself has got to be at least as improbable. God is the ultimate Boeing 747" (114). Another way of putting this is "who made God?" or "how did God happen?"

Put another way,

> Any God capable of designing a universe, carefully and foresightfully tuned to lead to our evolution [or to create it, straight up (DW)], must be a supremely complex and improbable entity who needs an even bigger explanation than the one he is supposed to provide. (147)

Or yet another way, "The designer hypothesis immediately raises the larger problem of who designed the designer" (158).

Got that? This is the argument that answers the implied question in the title of this chapter, "Why There Almost Certainly Is No God." Let me answer briefly, with two responses in ascending order of importance. First, Dawkins's argument depends upon God being *complicated*, like a universe-making machine would have to be. Now we accept the inference that God must be *greater* than the universe He made, and that He must be infinite, and omnipotent, certainly. But Dawkins spends a good bit of time in this chapter trying (unsuccessfully) to resist a central claim about God that Christians have made for centuries, i.e., that God is simple.

For a glimpse of the historic teaching of Christians on this, let me refer to the online *Stanford Encyclopedia of Philosophy*.

> According to the classical theism of Augustine, Anselm, Aquinas and their adherents, God is radically unlike creatures in that he is devoid of any complexity or composition, whether physical or metaphysical. Besides lacking spatial and temporal parts, God is free of matter-form composition, potency-act composition, and existence-essence composition. There is also no real distinction between God as subject of his attributes and his attributes. God is thus in a sense requiring clarification *identical* to each of his attributes, which implies that each attribute is identical to every other one. God is omniscient, then, not in virtue of instantiating or exemplifying omniscience—which would imply a real distinction between God and the property of omniscience—but by *being* omniscience. And the same holds for each of the divine omni-attributes: God IS what he *has*. As identical to each of his attributes, God is identical to his nature. And since his nature or essence is identical to his existence, God is identical to his existence. This is the doctrine of divine simplicity (DDS). It is to be understood as an affirmation of God's absolute transcendence of creatures. God is not only radically

non-anthropomorphic, but radically non-creaturo-morphic, not only in respect of the properties he possesses, but in his manner of possessing them. God, we could say, differs in his very ontology from any and all created beings.[2]

I don't want to act as though an encyclopedia of philosophy is an arbiter of orthodoxy (even though there is a lot of really cool stuff in that definition). My point is simply a historic one. Dawkins's argument depends upon God's complexity, and this means his argument doesn't apply at all to the triune God of the Christian faith, because Christians have claimed for many centuries that God is not complicated in the way that Dawkins's argument requires. Alvin Plantinga does a really fine job dissecting Dawkins at this point in a review of *The God Delusion* in Books and Culture.[3]

My second response is related to this point but looks at it from a few steps farther away. God is I am that I am. The child's question, "What did God stand on when He made the world?" is a question that presupposes that God is a contingent being like we are instead of the necessary being that the Bible claims He is. Christians do not just claim that God is *there*, we also claim that He is there *as a particular kind of being*. God's

2. William F. Vallicella, "African Sage Philosophy," in *Stanford Encyclopedia of Philosophy*. Stanford University, 1997–. Article published March 20, 2006; last modified January 2, 2015. https://plato.stanford.edu/archives/spr2016/entries/divine-simplicity/.

3. Which you can find at https://www.booksandculture.com/articles/2007/marapr/1.21.html.

aseity (another theological term) means that His existence does not require explanation. God's existence is necessary; He requires no explanation beyond Himself. His existence (unlike our own) does not depend upon anything outside Himself. He is what He is.

Now as much as he would like to, Dawkins cannot have a problem with aseity as such—it is another "not whether but which." It is not *whether* you are going to believe in something that is self-existent, it is *which* entity you are going to believe is self-existent. In answer to the philosopher's question, "Why is there something rather than nothing at all?" there are really only two directions to go. You can postulate the eternity of atoms banging around or the eternity of God—the aseity of matter and energy or the aseity of God. If you believe the former, the universe is eternal. If you believe the latter, only God is eternal, and He spoke the contingent universe into existence out of nothing, *ex nihilo*.

At some point, every worldview has to say "just because." In every worldview, someone is going to back you up against your ultimate wall, and you will say, "*this* just is." Dawkins believes that just-is-ness should be asserted about hydrogen, a colorless, odorless gas that, given enough time, eventually turns into Richard Dawkins, not to mention his opponents. But we believe it should be said, with glad reverence and joyful simplicity of heart, about God the Father Almighty, Maker of Heaven and Earth.

But I will give Dawkins this much: his argument *does* apply to the thesis that we were created by super smart space aliens. Of *them* it is reasonable to ask, "How did they get there?" But speaking of the triune God, it does not even begin to approach success as an argument that addresses anything at issue.

CHAPTER 8

WHO? ME?

R ichard Dawkins knows that he cannot just say
that religion is silly, and that people are silly
for believing it. Given his evolutionary premises, he has to give a *Darwinian* account of why people
are so overwhelmingly religious. This is the goal of his
next chapter in *The God Delusion.*

> Religion is so wasteful, so extravagant, and Darwinian
> selection habitually targets and eliminates waste. If
> a wild animal habitually performs some useless ac-
> tivity, natural selection will favour rival individuals
> who devote the time and energy, instead, to surviv-
> ing and reproducing. Nature cannot afford frivolous
> *jeux d'espirit.* Ruthless utilitarianism trumps, even if
> it doesn't always seem that way. (163)

That being the case, then what's with these churches, temples, synagogues, and whatnot all over the
place? Why did natural selection select *that* stuff? On
the surface, it would seem to be the bumper sticker
none of us has ever seen—not the Jesus fish eating the
Darwin fish with feet, but a big Darwin fish with feet
eating a little Darwin fish with feet, and leaving all the
little Jesus fish alone.

In other words, the preponderance of faith is an evolutionary fact, one that Dawkins knows he must explain. Now his explanation is long and involved, and
it is not really my purpose to engage with him at that
level. I simply want to commend him for noticing that,
on his premises, widespread religion was created by
an impersonal process that was favoring the fittest.
Dawkins gives several ways this could be explained,
and the one he favors is that the trait giving survival
advantages also throws off byproducts, religion being
one of those byproducts. In other words, the trait that
evolution would favor is children obeying their parents
and believing what they are told. This keeps kids out
of the woods, off the freeway, out of the medicine cab-
inet, and so on. But because kids who listen to their
parents will survive at a better rate than the kids who
are under the kitchen sink drinking the Drano, this
means that what also survives are the religious opinions and superstitions of the parents. But this is just a

byproduct, and this explanation is the one favored by Dawkins (172).

The way I want to answer Dawkins here is by pointing out how he has framed the question. Here I sit, Christian convictions bouncing around in my head, and Dawkins knows that this requires an explanation. Why have millions of years of evolutionary selection given us Arkansas Methodists, Brooklyn Jews, Saudi Muslims, and so on, *ad infinitum*. But in this book, the one set of convictions that requires no explanation at all would be (surprise!) atheism.

This is because Dawkins cannot afford to argue that his entire book was written the way it was because it is the result of impersonal forces grinding away. This would lead some readers to think that it might therefore not be *true*, and Dawkins obviously thinks that what he is writing is actually *true*. He believes what he believes because he has courageously followed the argument wherever it leads, and *we* believe the contrary because the cosmos is much larger than we are and has churned out a considerable number of intellectual blind alleys, down which we are chasing our blinkered lives.

In other words, Dawkins explains the convictions of his adversaries in terms of atoms banging around, and he explains his own convictions with a blithe confidence in the correspondence of the chemical reactions in his head to the actual state of affairs in the outside world. But what reason can we have for assuming that? The idea that someone could come to Christ as the result of following a line of reasoning seems never to have occurred to Dawkins. That's what *he* did. We don't get to do that.

But atheism requires an evolutionary explanation every bit as much as religious conviction does. And that explanation cannot appeal to the correspondence of the chemical reactions in the head to the events of the outside world—what a contrived business *that* would be. Given atheistic principles, we have no reason to assign any truth value to any arrangements of materials. Dawkins's atheism in his head no more aligns to any actual "no-Godness" out there than the waving of the blades of grass in a really big meadow are busy formulating the next big advance in quantum physics. Evolution occasionally allows atheists to develop, but this is *a complete accident*, and their existence cannot be justified by the convergence of their opinions to the facts of the case. Rather, the facts of the case require us to believe that all atheists have struck on "the truth" completely at random. It might be so, but that is not why they think so.

Dawkins's lack of epistemological self-awareness is nowhere more evident than here. He is the enlightened one. We are the ones in darkness. He explains our darkness completely. But given that explanation, he is just as much in the darkness. And not only will he not explain where he got the magic flashlight, he will not admit that he *has* a magic flashlight.

He offers an evolutionary explanation of a particular form of intellectual development, serenely unaware of how that explanation applies just as much to him as to anyone else. The thought never crosses his mind. But I can't fault him for this really. If he is (accidentally) right, there is no such thing as a mind to cross.

CHAPTER 9

SCRATCHING THE ITCH OF MORALITY

I n the next chapter, Richard Dawkins undertakes the question of morality, seeking to ground that morality on the unshakable foundation of evolution. What kind of foundation might that be? Well, let's go down into the basement and have ourselves a little check.

But before getting to this important issue, Dawkins gives us some samples of the hate mail he and other atheists receive. In order to really engage with your religious adversaries, it is important to understand them, and quote representative spokesmen accurately and fairly. You really want to pick the most able adversaries so that no one can accuse you of cherry-picking your opponents. That is no doubt the principle behind Dawkins's selection of fellow Oxfordian Alister McGrath to represent the opposition. Just kidding.

> Satan worshiping scum . . . Please die and go to hell
> . . . I hope you get a painful disease like rectal cancer
> and die a slow painful death, so you can meet your
> God, SATAN . . . Hey dude this freedom from religion
> thing sux . . . So you fags and dykes take it easy and
> watch where you go cuz wheneer you least expect
> it god will get you . . . If you don't like this country
> and what it was founded on & for, get the f*** out
> of it and go straight to hell . . . PS. F*** you, you
> communist whore . . . Get your black asses out of the
> U.S.A.   You are without excuse. Creation is more
> than enough evidence of the LORD JESUS CHRIST'S
> omnipotent power. (212–213)

Apparently Christian apologetics has three schools of thought: evidentialism, presuppositionalism, and scurrilous antinomian abuse.

Dawkins wants us to realize that religious believers think that belief in God is really, *really* important and essential and nonnegotiable when it comes to grounding morality in something other than humanistic brain fog. But Dawkins is ready for us and seeks to show us that we have a scientific (read, evolutionary) basis that accounts for our feelings of moral sentiments.

> We now have four good Darwinian reasons for individuals to be altruistic, generous or 'moral' towards

each other. First, there is the special case of genetic kindship. Second, there is reciprocation: the repayment of favours given, and the giving of favours in 'anticipation' of payback. Following on from this there is, third, the Darwinian benefit of acquiring a reputation for generosity and kindness. And fourth, if Zahavi is right, there is the particular additional benefit of conspicuous generosity as a way of buying unfakeably authentic advertising. (219–220)

Dawkins compares the altruistic urges we have to our sexual impulses. The fact that the original reasons for their formation may be missing now does not keep us from feeling them. He points out (obviously) that the sexual urges were programmed into us (back in our baboonlike stage) in order to further the propagation of children, or, as the mother baboon might say affectionately, yard apes. He then points out that a modern couple can know that the woman is infertile (because she is on the pill, say) and yet this does not make the sexual desire go away (221).

> I am suggesting that the same is true of the urge to kindness—to altruism, to generosity, to empathy, to pity. In ancestral times, we had the opportunity to be altruistic only towards close kin and potential reciprocators. Nowadays that restriction is no longer there, but the rule of thumb persists. Why would it not? It is just like sexual desire Both are misfirings, Darwinian mistakes: blessed, previous mistakes. (221)

In other words, back when we lived in villages, just down from the trees, the promotion of our own genetic offspring, the rules of reciprocity, reputation issues, and ways of showing dominance were all crucial to survival, so natural selection favored them all. Today, it might be the case that none of these things applies to some anonymous resident of some big city, but that doesn't keep him from feeling empathy when he sees a fitting object of compassion. Just as a man might lust after a woman he knows to be infertile, so another man might feel compassion toward someone with no connection to his genes at all.

So, okay, I follow all this. But this simply accounts for the *existence* of my moral sentiments. It gives me no reason at all to *obey* them. Just as a man might know that sexual desire was evolution's way of propagating those critical and irreplaceable genes of his, and yet decide to live in a way that thwarts this intent (getting a vasectomy, for example), so another man might know that his feelings of compassion are, at the end of the day, just feelings. If he goes with them, fine, if not, equally fine. What authority does the genetic residue of ancient village life actually have? It may have explanatory power with regard to my moral feelings, but it can have no imperatival authority. If one man wants to go with his feelings and show compassion and kindness, then why not? Scratch what itches. But if he doesn't want to drift with his feelings and wants instead to discipline himself contrary to the known evolutionary reasons for having the feelings, why shouldn't he?

Dawkins says that our moral sentiments are just like our sexual desires. We can know that the reasons for having the desires are obsolete, and yet we still have them. This misses two crucial points. The first is that the existence of sexual desire brings with it no moral imperative to *have* a sexual desire or to have it directed in fruitful directions. So if a man desires to redirect his sexual desire, or if he castrates himself in order to pursue some other end, there is no reason (located *in* the sexual desire itself) that can provide any direction in making such choices. Evolution provides the *is*, it has nothing whatever to say about the *ought*. But if our feelings of altruism and compassion are exactly the same kind of thing, then if the vast bulk of the human species, when feeling this way, decides to be nice, that is just fine. And if others decide to go the sociopathic route, well then, equally fine. Of course, we might decide to hang all the sociopaths on utilitarian grounds, but that is just a matter of keeping order—keeping the sewers working, the electrical grid up, and the homicidal lunatics off the street. Not really a question of morality.

But this leads to the second question. We want to be careful about killing too many of the sociopaths because we must never forget the next big jump in evolution. Natural selection is still ongoing, so we want to be wary about killing the mutants. Might be a tad uncomfortable for us moral dinosaurs for a time, but hey, progress is always like that. In other words, if speciation is still occurring, then why shouldn't big city anonymity have its crack at programming the future just like small village closeness had its shot? But Dawkins is way too much of a sentimentalist to swallow any of these reductios. No, he wants to settle in permanently with his nice, cozy morality, the fruit of those "blessed, previous mistakes," and just keep things the way they are, with everybody being nice to each other.

But the question won't go away. *Why?* What do you say to the person who disputes all this and wants to do whatever he wants to do, milk of human kindness be damned? And when you say it to him, why should he listen to you? Hume posited a chasm between *is* and *ought*, and Dawkins has not only *not* engineered a bridge across the chasm, but his attempts appear to consist almost entirely of "Gee, wouldn't it be nice if we had a bridge here?"

At first Dawkins says that the notion that we "need God to be good" is just plain crass—as though Christians are only capable of being good as long as the celestial surveillance camera is pointed in our direction. And of course, if that is what we are doing, it would be crass. But then Dawkins really surprised me for the first time in this book. He stepped away from the caricatures, and actually represented the views of a hypothetical (and capable) Christian apologist. The point is not that we will only be good if someone is watching, but rather that, in the absence of a transcendental moral absolute, we have no way of telling whether we are being good or not. He indulged in the caricature for several pages, but then he gave an effective answer to all that. At first, we were all in a room with the rules clearly posted, and then the sky camera was taken away, and there was no way to tell who had kept the rules or not. In this setting, the Christians were clearly only giving eyeservice, to use the language of the apostle Paul. But then a real response from Christians was anticipated. Suppose that not only the camera is taken away, but so are the posted rules. No one is told to do anything, one way or the other, no one is watching, and we are all trying to cheer ourselves up with nebulous notions of altruism while milling around confusedly in the room with no name. Now what?

To his credit, Dawkins actually raises this potent objection to his argument. But then, in a lame way, he doesn't answer it at all. He brings up Kant's categorical imperative, says that it seems to work for some things like truth-telling, but not for other stuff, and then tells us that "moral philosophers are the professionals when it comes to thinking about right and wrong" (232). And it turns out that they divide into two camps—the deontologists, who think that morality consists of doing one's duty, and the consequentialists, who think that actions should be evaluated for their morality on the basis of their consequences. Oh. So what does natural selection have to say about deontology and consequentialism? And, most importantly, *why?* Nothing at all, apparently. Dawkins then lamely concludes the chapter by pointing out that patriotism can generate a close approximation of moral absolutism. Okay, not to the mention the last refuge of the scoundrel. But we still have been given no information about what constitutes a moral choice or action. Which option does Dawkins take and why? He can't just wave his hands over the ethical conundrum and move on to the next chapter. But that is what he does.

CHAPTER 10

PIÑA COLADAS AND GETTING CAUGHT IN THE RAIN

The next chapter in Dawkins is called "The 'Good' Book and the Changing Moral *Zeitgeist*," and it is one of the strangest bits of business I have encountered in some time.

The first part of the chapter is dedicated to proving how the Bible exhibits "sheer strangeness" and is "just plain weird" (237). To establish this, he tells a number of Bible stories—Abraham passing Sarah off as his sister, Jephthah's daughter, the Levite's concubine, Lot sleeping with his daughters, and so on. He does this

283

in order to prove that no one, not even the most conservative Christian, gets his morality from the Bible. Getting your morality "from the Bible," for Dawkins, apparently consists of justifying any action provided it can be shown to have occurred somewhere in the pages of Scripture. And since no one, not even the most rigorous follower of the courtship model, sets a bride price for his daughter at a hundred Philistine foreskins, we must all of us be really inconsistent. "You *say* you believe the Bible . . ."

Dawkins's knowledge of scriptural hermeneutics and the nature of unfolding revelation is frankly sophomoric, and that constitutes a gratuitous insult to sophomores. The only alternative that he can imagine to slavish imitation of anything done by any given Bible character is to relegate the Bible to the world of "symbolism." But if you do *that*, he argues, the Bible becomes a nose of wax, and anybody can make it say anything he wants. Those are the two alternatives presented by Dawkins in this chapter—wooden imitation or up-for-grabs symbolism.

But there are plenty of people who take Judges as literal history who do not believe that carving a dead concubine into pieces as a summons to war is righteous. We believe in this way, not because the incident offends our modern moral sensibilities (which it does), but because the text itself leads us to this conclusion. The text is the *basis* for our modern moral sensibilities. This was a time in Israel's history when "every man did that which was right in his own eyes," and the results were frequently appalling.

Dawkins clearly does not know how to read a literary collection of texts like the Bible, and it is equally clear that there is an entire *world* of literary and biblical scholarship out there from which, if it had a deadly contagious disease, Dawkins would be quite safe.

Suppose that *Macbeth* were a sacred text. According to Dawkins, *either* you would have to go out to find yourself a Duncan to kill (in order to "get your morality" from Shakespeare), or you would have to interpret the whole thing as a series of nebulous symbols. "Nope. No other options." Good grief.

Having set up this wobbly foundation, Dawkins proceeds to get even wobblier. Where do we get our morality? Since he has shown (!) that nobody gets his morality from the Bible, where *do* we get our morality? At this point I have to do what Dave Barry frequently does and assure my readers that I am not making this up. We get our morality from the contemporary *zeitgeist*, or spirit of the age. Everybody, more or less, has the same basic morality, the one notable exception (kind of) being the conservative Christians in the U.S. who are busy making up the American Taliban. But we all have a basic sense of what constitutes good and what constitutes bad. Dawkins cites a list of commandments he got off the internet that illustrates this, called the "New Ten Commandments." It would be exceedingly tedious to cite them all, but I will quote some of them, along with one I made up. See if you can tell which one *that* is.

2. In all things, strive to cause no harm.

5. Live life with a sense of joy and wonder.

6. Always seek to be learning something new.

10. Question everything.

11. Love piña coladas and getting caught in the rain.

Okay, so I added the last one. But I think you could only tell because it was supposed to be ten commandments, and that had an eleven by it. And what is it with that number ten? Question *everything* except for stupid, arbitrary lists like this one. Whenever I see that bumper sticker that says "Question Authority," I want to get a marker pen and write on it, "Don't tell *me* what to do."

But Dawkins celebrates the *zeitgeist*. He points to the suffrage of women as an example of this *zeitgeist*, with women gaining the right to vote in New Zealand in 1893, Britain in 1928, Switzerland in 1971, and in Kuwait in 2006. See? Look at us go.

Dawkins is jubilant because "the *Zeitgeist* moves on" (267). "The *Zeitgeist* moves on, so inexorably that we sometimes take it for granted and forget that the change is a real phenomenon in its own right" (267).

Dawkins is driving the car, and I am in the backseat trying to figure out what I thought were MapQuest directions, but the night was foggy and really dark. Later I discovered that the MapQuest directions were actually grease stains from a piece of pizza left on one of Dawkins's scientific papers.

"How are we doing?" say I, somewhat worried.

"Great, great," he cheerfully replies.

"Where are we going again?" I want to know.

"We are making excellent time!" he answers. "Never better!"

"How do you know that?" I want to know.

"Look at all the other cars zipping along right beside us," he says. "Zeitgeisting down the road like crazy."

In other words, we don't know where we are, where we are going, who made the car, or who gave us the keys, but we are making excellent time nonetheless. I don't have a copy of it with me, but it reminds me of C.S. Lewis's wonderful hymn to evolution. "Lead us, evolution, lead us/Up the future's endless stair/Chop us, change us, prod us, weed us/Lead us, goodness, who knows where."

"The shift is in a recognizably consistent direction, which most of us would judge as improvement" (268). Most of us, hey? Or is that just most of the smart ones? And does that *make* it an improvement? Can "most of us" be wrong? If not, doesn't that open the door to all manner of hellish dystopias? And if so, by what standard? Is a majority vote an all-purpose disinfectant?

Begging the question like a champion, Dawkins simply assumes what he needs to prove. The *Zeitgeist* is doing good things as long as it is moving in a "progressive" direction. But how on earth are we supposed to define *progress*?

"The *Zeitgeist* may move, and move in a generally progressive direction, but as I have said it is a sawtooth not a smooth improvement, and there have been some appalling reversals" (272). Appalling reversals? By what standard? A generally progressive direction? By what standard? Improvement? By what standard? The standard for how fast and in what direction the car *should* go cannot be how fast and in what direction the car is *currently* going. A car is not a map. An internal combustion engine is not a map. But Dawkins dismisses all this with a facile, "Look at us go."

And the interesting thing is that, in the first part of the chapter, when he was arguing against Christians who pick and choose from their Bibles (which would be bad, I agree, if we were doing it), he demonstrated plainly that he understands this principle. When he was talking about what parts of the Bible we should follow and what parts not, he laid down a principle that is quite good. I am glad that he did this because he shows that he understands the principle *clearly*.

Now all he has to do is apply it to himself. But, son of a gun, he doesn't get around to that.

> Remember, all I am trying to establish for the moment is that we do not, as a matter of fact, derive our morals from scripture. Or, if we do, we pick and choose among the scriptures for the nice bits and reject the nasty. *But then we must have some independent criterion for deciding which are the moral bits:* a criterion which, wherever it comes from, cannot come from scripture itself and is presumably available to all of us whether we are religious or not. (243, emphasis cheerfully and helpfully added by DW)

According to Dawkins, there are competing moral claims in the Bible. There aren't, but let's give it to him for a moment. He says that in order to make a choice, we must have a criterion of choosing. That's right, we do need that. Now, there are also competing moral claims out there in Zeitgeistland, and Dawkins knows it. I mean, Dawkins just cannot get over the lunatic theocracy that Americans are busy building under that renowned theocrat George W. Bush. *That,* surely, is a contrary wind to the prevailing winds of progressivism. So let us change our metaphor from driving a car aimlessly to windsurfing aimlessly, because the *zeitgeist* is more like a stiff wind than it is like a road just lying there. Dawkins wants us to windsurf in a particular direction, in front of what he thinks ought to be the prevailing winds. But why should we care what he thinks the prevailing winds *ought* to be? What matters is what they *are*, right?

But then Dawkins gives the game away. It all boils down to personal choice.

> Of course, irritated theologians will protest that we don't take the book of Genesis literally anymore. But that is my whole point! We pick and choose which bits of scripture to believe, which bits to write off as symbols or allegories. Such picking and choosing is a matter of personal decision, *just as much, or as little, as the atheist's decision to follow this moral precept or that was a personal decision, with-out an absolute foundation.* If one of these is 'morality flying by the seat of its pants,' so is the other. (238, again, the emphasis is cheerfully mine as I attempt to clarify these issues)

I agree that if they are both flying by the seat of their pants, then they both are. But if Christians are following a sure word from God, a light in a dark place, that does not change what Dawkins is doing. Dawkins here acknowledges that, whatever else is the case, he is flying by the seat of his pants. How does one answer any perplexing ethical questions? *Personal choice* trumps all. Should I believe in science? Personal choice. Should I accept the theory of evolution? Personal choice. Should I adopt a progressive political agenda? Personal choice. Should I participate in hate crimes against homosexuals? Personal choice. Should I support apartheid? Personal choice. Should I support the expansion of the American empire? Personal choice. Should I accept the authority of reason and evidence? Personal choice. Should I ditch my wife for some new babe I thought I found? Personal choice. Should I find Intelligent Design compelling? Personal choice. Should I help the old lady across the street? Personal choice. Push her into the traffic? Personal choice. Should I vote for the presidential candidate most likely to outlaw abortion? Personal choice. Should I give my selfish genes more of a shot at immortality by becoming a serial rapist? Personal choice. Should I respect the personal choices of others? Personal choice. Should I have nothing but contempt for the personal choices of others? Personal choice.

Dawkins has written enough in this chapter to reveal that he knows what he is doing. But at the same time, it is also clear that he is still half ashamed of it.

CHAPTER 11

RABBITLESS ROCKS

I n the next chapter, Dawkins seeks to answer the question, "Why are you so hostile?" So believers in God are delusional. So what? Why get that datum wound tight around your axle?

He also has to explain why, given his adversarial stance toward Christianity and creationism, "I never take part in debates with creationists." With regard to this, he records the deliciously snarky response from a scientific colleague who replies to creationist invitations to debate with this: "That would look great on your CV; not so good on mine" (281). More on this shortly.

Dawkins tries to answer the charge that he is an atheistic fundamentalist because of his obvious belligerence. He is part of a new "militant atheism" that has a clear take-no-prisoners approach. Is this not a fundamentalist mindset? Dawkins says *no*.

> I am no more fundamentalist when I say evolution is true than when I say it is true that New Zealand is in the southern hemisphere. We believe in evolution because the evidence supports it, and we would abandon it overnight if new evidence arose to disprove it. (282)

This comment is strange on two counts. First, on the question of hemispheres, consider an illustration in favor of "consciousness raising" that Dawkins used earlier in the book.

> That is where consciousness raising comes in. It is for a deeper reason than gimmicky fun that, in Australia and New Zealand, you can buy maps of the world with the South Pole on top. What splendid consciousness-raisers those maps would be, pinned to the walls of our northern hemisphere classrooms. Day after day, the children would be reminded that 'north' is an arbitrary polarity which has no monopoly on 'up.' The map would intrigue them as well as raise their consciousness. (115)

Arbitrary polarity. Exactly so. And this applies to more than *north* and *south*. This is what all the T's and F's in a truth tree are, given atheism—arbitrary polarities. Dawkins keeps trying to raise his consciousness, but he keeps bumping his head on the ceiling. He wants objective truth when it suits him, and he wants consciousness-raising relativism when it suits him. If this seems like a contradiction, that's okay. He's raising his consciousness.

This brings us to the second point. Dawkins says that evolution would be abandoned overnight if evidence were brought forward that disproved it. But how can we know if the evidence is any good? You know, like *solid* evidence? Well, anything that would bring about the rejection of evolution is, you know, bogus on the face of it. How can we be "truth at all costs" scientists and hedge our bets at the same time?

"When challenged by a zealous Popperian to say how evolution could ever be falsified, J.B.S. Haldane famously growled: 'Fossil rabbits in the Precambrian.' No such anachronistic fossils have ever been authentically found..." (128). One word in there cracks me up and gives the whole game away: "*authentically* found." This is a great challenge and sounds very bold—until you realize that Precambrian rock is *defined* as being rabbitless. No such evidence has ever been *authentically* found. What my net don't catch ain't fish. "*That* can't be a Precambrian rock. Got a rabbit in it, for Pete's sake.*"

This goes back to the refusal to debate creationists mentioned earlier. Exactly how open to hearing alternative evidence might Dawkins be? As it turns out, not at all. He won't debate creationists, even though in this chapter he mentions one creationist scientist,

Kurt Wise, whose scientific craft competence is undisputed. But he is mentioned as a pathetic casualty of religion because he continues to believe the Bible, despite having been trained under Stephen Jay Gould. "I am hostile to religion because of what it did to Kurt Wise" (286). Why not debate Kurt Wise? The snarky CVs comment wouldn't apply here, now would it?

Another reason that Dawkins is on the warpath is because of the nutcases in the Muslim world and in "the incipient American theocracy" (286).

> In the United States of recent years the phrase 'American Taliban' was begging to be coined, and a swift Google search nets more than a dozen websites that have done so. (288)

> The ambition to achieve what can only be called a Christian fascist state is entirely typical of the American Taliban. (292)

The farther the reader goes in this book, the more one suspects that Dawkins has been relying on Google way more than a scholar should. It really doesn't take much to google up the hyperventilations of hysterical liberals, and a Brit like Dawkins might easily come to believe that men like Randall Terry and Paul Hill are representative leaders of conservative Christians in America. And that, in fact, is what he does (292–296). This is great for whipping up the moonbats, but it has little to do with what is actually occurring here.

Another reason for Dawkins's stridency is the fact that conservative believers have been fighting for a respect for human life, born and unborn. But Dawkins complains that prolifers frequently support the death penalty.

> Human embryos are examples of human life. Therefore, by absolutist religious lights, abortion is simply wrong: full-fledged murder. I am not sure what to make of my admittedly anecdotal observation that many of those who most ardently oppose the taking of embryonic life also seem to be more than usually enthusiastic about taking adult life. (291)

Take me, for instance. I support the death penalty for convicted murderers, and I oppose the death penalty for unborn children. "Ha! Caught you! Wiggle out of *that* one!" If someone has forfeited their right to life through an outrageous crime on another, and that person is given a fair and complete trial, then executing them is an act of *justice*. If someone has not done such an act, and they are given no trial or hearing whatever, then executing them is an act of *injustice*. This is a real puzzler for Dawkins. Trial? Justice? Innocence? Guilt? Injustice? These are strange concepts. I must hear more about this religion of yours.

Dawkins is not opposed to abortion because a small cluster of human cells, however *human* they might be, do not have a nervous system. "An early embryo has the sentience, as well as the semblance, of a tadpole"

(297). And for some arbitrary reason, the ability to suffer pain is the ethical measuring rod Dawkins has decided to use. In an attempt to be consistent, he calls for more humane treatment of animals in slaughter-houses, who can suffer more pain than an early embryo does. But if this is how we run the calculus, then can we not achieve consistency in the other direction as well? What would Dawkins say about the murder of a heroin addict with no family, one who would never be missed, provided that murder were conducted pain-lessly? The future pain that the addict would no doubt experience is all avoided, and no pain is experienced in the experience of death itself. If the do-gooder sneaks up on him while asleep, he doesn't even have the pain of fearful anticipation. The action would certainly cause an overall reduction of pain in one nervous sys-tem and no additional pain in any others. And that's what counts, right? All about nervous systems, right?

CHAPTER 12

IN THE ZONE

The ninth chapter of Dawkins's book is entitled "Childhood, Abuse, and the Escape from Religion." The chapter is almost impudent in its intellectual dishonesty, and more than impudent in its proposal.

Dawkins begins by telling a heart-wrenching story from nineteenth-century Italy, in which a young Jewish boy, Edgardo Mortara, had been secretly baptized by his babysitter. When this was discovered, the Inquisition required that he be removed from his parents and brought up in a Catholic home, which then happened. "It passes all sensible understanding, but they sincerely believed they were doing him a good turn by taking him away from his parents and giving him a Christian upbringing. They felt a duty of *protection*" (313).

As Dawkins writes about this, every sensible reader is right with him. This was an appalling thing to do and is surpassed only by Dawkins telling this story as an introduction to HIS proposal to do precisely the same kind of thing. He professes astonishment that these nineteenth-century Catholics felt a duty to protect this young boy from being raised a Jew. He then serenely passes on to his subsequent argument that we moderns have a duty to protect young children everywhere from being raised by religious people who consider it their duty to raise their child in their faith. Dawkins's real problem is apparently that not *enough* children were removed from their homes. If Dawkins or his editor had not been in the grip of their smugitudinous secularism, they would have seen the glaring contradiction in this chapter. When it comes to lack of self-awareness, in this particular argument Dawkins was in the zone. Dawkins begins his chapter by grossing us all out with a story about how some people several centuries ago ate some cockroaches. He then makes this the foundation of his argument for eating centipedes instead. And he does not see that this is what he is doing. The title to the chapter contains the word *abuse*. And this is the hinge of Dawkins's proposal. Parents who teach their children so that they share their parents' faith are, according to Dawkins, *abusive* parents. Dawkins thinks he can make this charge and remain tolerant because it is okay with him if the parents want to be Christians (gee, thanks!), but if they baptize their children, or provide them with a Christian education, or both, then they are not to be considered Christian parents, but rather abusive parents.

> Even without physical abduction, isn't it always a form of child abuse to label children as possessors of beliefs that they are too young to have thought about? Yet the practice continues to this day, almost entirely unquestioned. (315)

And what do you *do* with abusive parents? Well, you make them stop. And if they won't stop, then you remove the child from that home in order to protect them—just like what happened to little Edgardo. Coming at this from another angle, as horrible as the sexual abuse of children by priests might be, Dawkins says, "the damage was arguably less than the long-term psychological damage inflicted by bringing the child up Catholic in the first place" (317). So not only is providing children with a religious upbringing abuse, but it is arguably worse kind of abuse than sexual abuse.

It is not a crime, according to Dawkins, to be a Christian in the presence of your children, at least for the present, but it is a crime to bring them up in the nurture and admonition of the Lord.

> I am persuaded that the phrase 'child abuse' is no exaggeration where used to describe what teachers and

priests are doing to children whom they encourage to believe in something like the punishment of unshriven mortal sins in an eternal hell. (318)

And Dawkins favorably quotes a colleague, Nicholas Humphrey, who delivered *this* for our consideration:

> So we should no more allow parents to teach their children to believe, for example, in the literal truth of the Bible or that the planets rule their lives than we should allow parents to knock their children's teeth out or lock them in a dungeon. (326)

So far, such abuse would include baptizing infants, teaching children about God's judgment of the human race and the fact that the Bible is the Word of God, and having them memorize verses to recite in the annual Christmas pageant. All these things are, by definition, child abuse. And decent society has a duty to protect children from child abuse, does it not? Get those kids out of there—just like the Catholics did with Edgardo.

Humphrey (and Dawkins) were both appalled at the multicultural reaction to the discovery of the body of a young Inca girl, the Peruvian Ice Maiden, who had apparently been killed in a ritual sacrifice. All the usual progressive suspects were gushing over the fact that in *her* culture "being selected for the signal honour of being sacrificed" (327) was an honor indeed. But Humphrey says that the Ice Maiden thought this way only because she didn't know the scientific facts about the material universe. If *he* had brought her up and gotten her a proper education, she wouldn't have thought the way she did, and she wouldn't have wanted to be sacrificed. This is quite true—she wouldn't have wanted that if she had been brought up in a conservative Christian home either. But it is also beside the point.

The myth of neutrality has both Humphrey and Dawkins by the throat. They want to protect all the children of the world from the abuse of their parents' religious opinions, and the standard they propose for evaluating all the opinions of all these parents are the indisputable facts that make up *their* worldview. As Popeye would say, what a coinkydink. This is because they are *right*, darn it, just like the nineteenth-century Catholics. And, incredibly, they cannot see that this is what they are doing.

> The Inca priests cannot be blamed for their ignorance, and it could perhaps be thought harsh to judge them stupid and puffed up. But they can be blamed for foisting their own beliefs on as child too young to decide whether to worship the sun or not. (328)

But the Christian belief is that the Incan priests *should* be blamed for their ignorance, because they were suppressing the truth about God in their unrighteousness and were worshiping a lie. The way to deal with this is through preaching the gospel to them, calling upon them to repent and forsake their idols. But the Dawkins approach is breathtaking. *His* proposal, if we want to dignify it with such a name, is to have all the parents in the world—Christian, Muslim, Jews, Buddhists, and so on—to be required to raise their children the way *Dawkins* would, and then, when they are eighteen (or whatever), they can become whatever religion they want, provided it is not a religion that has anything like infant baptism in it.

"Charming? Heart-warming? No, it is not, it is neither; it is grotesque. How could any decent person think it right to label four-year-old children with the cosmic and theological opinions of their parents?" (337–338). The implication here is that children are all wards of the state, which must be secular. Your children are not yours. This is more than the separation of church and state; it is the separation of church and children. It is not a separation of the state and children.

"Please, please raise your consciousness about this, and raise the roof whenever you hear it happening. A child is not a Christian child, not a Muslim child, but a child of Christian parents or a child of Muslim parents" (339). No, thanks. Not going to do it. I said a moment ago that Dawkins does not see that he is demanding that all worldviews defer to his. Because he is right, and because everyone else is wrong, children must be removed from homes (or not) on his principles. He will brook no dispute or discussion on the point. The scientist worldview is right, and evolution is right, and children must be removed from homes where

Dawkins-think is not properly taught. One of the reasons for doing this is that Dawkins was appalled by an instance in nineteenth-century Italy where a child was removed from a home where Catholic-think was not properly taught. I have honestly never seen anything like this in a book that people were taking seriously. And Dawkins teaches at *Oxford*.

But I don't fault Dawkins for insisting that law should be based on the worldview that he considers to be correct. What else should he think? That is not where his problem is. All law is imposed morality, and everyone who has a morality believes that the law should be based on that morality which is correct. This is what everybody does, and it is inescapable. Nobody wants to impose a morality that he believes to be a false morality and actually immoral.

The problem is that Dawkins doesn't know that he is doing this. He is unaware of the fact that he is looking out at the world through his own eyeballs, and his worldview, freighted with all kinds of radical assumptions, is simply invisible to him. What *he* sees is simply what "is," and what *others* see is the result of inexplicable superstitions. And we gotta get their children out of there.

This comes up in another way in this chapter. Dawkins has heard about a group of Christians who want public policy to reflect what *they* believe to be correct. Dawkins acts like he has never heard of such a thing. The ideer! *Them?* "If I had wanted to interview real extremists by modern American standards, I'd have gone for Reconstructionists whose 'Dominion Theology' openly advocates a Christian theocracy in America" (319).

An American colleague writes him in breathless excitement: "Europeans need to know there is a traveling theo-freak show . . . If secularists are not vigilant, Dominionists and Reconstructionists will soon be mainstream in a true American theocracy" (319).

In the first place, judging from the terminology being used here, Dawkins's intelligence-gathering is about twenty years out of date. In the second place, to report this as though the recons will be taking over tomorrow if the secularists are not capital-V vigilant is an exercise in capital-H hyperbole. But let us not get hung up on that kind of stuff, and just point out that all cultures reflect the central *cultus*. All cultures are embodied religion. Dawkins wants to have his religion be the basis for all public morality and law. Good for him. So do we. He doesn't believe in Jesus and wants that unbelief enshrined in the public square. We believe in Jesus and want His Lordship to be recognized in the public square. Of course there are some differences, based on the different nature of the worldviews represented. For example, I wouldn't want to have a Christian state kidnap kids from atheist homes, and he does want a secular state to kidnap Christian kids from Christian homes. But although our moralities differ, we both want those moralities to form the basis of the surrounding culture.

Dawkins steadfastly refuses to recognize the *situated* nature of his own knowledge. Because he denies the one true God, the only one who has immediate (nonmediated) knowledge of all things, Dawkins has volunteered to fill that vacancy himself. *He* will know things immediately, and he will know them without corruption. And from that pristine vantage point, he will give the order to have our kids taken away from us and raised in an antiseptic and scientific way. God deliver us.

CHAPTER 13

A BOWL OF SAWDUST PASTE

I n this last Dawkins installment, I want to do two things. The first is to briefly summarize his last chapter and respond to it. The second task is to develop something I mentioned in an earlier post—viz., that Dawkins is more than half ashamed of what he is doing—and for good reason.

This last chapter can be divided into two portions. The first part addresses issues like the power of religion to console. "What have you to offer the dying patients, the weeping bereaved, the lonely Eleanor Rigbys for whom God is their only friend?" (352).

Dawkins responds to this by pointing out, quite rightly, "Religion's power to console doesn't make it true" (352). Of course not—a doctor could console a terminally ill patient by lying to him and telling him he is going to get better. Lies that offer good news can console along with truths that actually are good news. Quite right. False gods can be a consolation just as the true God can be.

But there is a deeper question. Why does the human creature *need* consolation? A desperate longing thirst in the desert doesn't turn every mirage into water. But surely it argues that there is such a thing *as* water. Why would natural selection develop such an odd dead end? It would be as though we were all thirsty in a world without water, or hungry in a world without food, or full of sexual desire in a world without another sex, and so on. When we long for consolation, Dawkins tells us that it need not be God that we are longing for. He probably isn't there, and so we should just deal with it. All right. What is it that we are longing for? And why does atheism fail, in a spectacular way, to address this particular need? Scripture says that God has placed eternity in our hearts, which accounts for this longing for the transcendent. But in Dawkins's account, this longing is entirely illusory, and so he offers us something else. But why does that something else fail to satisfy? It is as though I am fainting from thirst because I want to drink from one of the brooks cascading off one of Heaven's mountains, and Dawkins offers me a bowl of sawdust paste instead.

Dawkins is capable of fine description in his writing, and in the second part of this final chapter, he sets out to tout the marvels of the sawdust paste. He tries to generate a lofty feeling of awe in us by describing various aspects of the physical universe in such a way as to make us say *whoa*.

> We try to visualize an electron as a tiny ball, in orbit around a larger cluster of balls representing protons and neutrons. That isn't what it is like at all. Electrons are not like little balls. They are not like anything we recognize. (363)

> Quantum mechanics, that rarefied pinnacle of twentieth-century scientific achievement, makes brilliantly successful predictions about the real world. (364–365)

> The entire dune walks across the desert in a westerly direction at a speed of about 17 metres per year. It retains its crescent shape and creeps along in the direction of the horns. (370)

> Could we, by training and practice, emancipate ourselves . . . and achieve some sort of intuitive—as well as just mathematical—understanding of the very small, the very large, and the very fast? I genuinely don't know the answer, but I am thrilled to be alive at a time when humanity is pushing against the limits

of understanding. Even better, we may eventually discover that there are no limits. (374)

No limits. And we shall be as God, knowing good and evil.

But the problem is that the religious need that human beings have, created as we have been in the image of God, cannot be satisfied by the pretensions or posturings of any idol. *Eternity* is in our hearts, and that longing cannot be filled by watching things go by us really fast, by becoming the most famous person in the world, by sacrificing a virgin in front of a stone idol, or by anything else that men may think up to do. If we understand that the created heavens and earth are a metaphor for the triune God who made them, we can be satisfied to hear of Him through His creation. The heavens declare the glory of God. Through the things that have been made, the divine majesty is announced to every sentient creature. But when His creation is severed from Him, as atheism seeks to do, all we have is a bunch of atoms banging around. And if we reflect a bit more, we realize this means that our thoughts are just the result of atoms banging around, which means in turn that we have no reason for trusting our thoughts. But *that* means we don't even know if there is such a thing as atoms banging around. Martin Luther famously took his stand because that is where God had led him, and his heart was captive to the Word of God.

Richard Dawkins takes his stand because he doesn't have anywhere to go.

And this leads to the broader point. Dawkins's college at Oxford, New College, was founded in 1379 by William Wykeham, Bishop of Winchester. In the endowment, he provided for ten chaplains, three clerks, and sixteen choristers. If the college income failed, they alone were to be retained. The purpose of the college was to provide for a place where people would be enabled to pray for the good bishop's soul (359).

> Today the college has only one chaplain and no clerks, and the steady century-by-century torrent of prayers for Wykeham in purgatory has dwindled to a trickle of two prayers per year. Even I feel a twinge of guilt, as a member of that Fellowship, for a trust betrayed. (359)

Dawkins tries to say this with a sense of ironic detachment, but he covers up his sense of unease unsuccessfully. It comes out in a number of places in the book.

"The present Astronomer Royal and President of the Royal Society, Martin Rees, told me that he goes to church as an 'unbelieving Anglican out of loyalty to the tribe'" (14). It is a loyalty that Dawkins wishes he could participate in, his wistfulness barely concealed.

"When I was a child and still carried a guttering torch for the Anglican Church" (261). In various places in the book, Dawkins refers to his Anglican upbringing, and in a number of places some sort of affection and yearning show through. At the end of chapter nine, he takes an odd turn, arguing for the retention of the Bible as a significant part of literary culture.

"But the main reason the English Bible needs to be part of our education is that it is a major source book for literary culture" (341). This is followed by almost two *pages* of phrases taken from the Bible that enrich our reading—phrases like "go to the ant," "physician heal thyself," "through a glass darkly," and so on.

Immediately after the list, Dawkins says one of the few things that I agreed with completely, not to mention enthusiastically: "P.G. Wodehouse is, for my money, the greatest writer of light comedy in English, and I bet fully half my list of biblical phrases will be found as allusions within his pages" (343). He has a point. My kids learned a great deal about the Bible from reading it themselves, and from church, but they also learned a good bit of it from Bertie Wooster who, as you should know, once won a prize for Scripture knowledge.

But this kind of affection is not sustained or consistent. The mask goes back on, and Dawkins is back to snarling about how the Bible is a pathological piece of work.

> And of course we can retain a sentimental loyalty to the cultural and literary traditions of, say, Judaism, Anglicanism, or Islam, and even participate in religious rituals such as marriages and funerals, without buying into the supernatural beliefs that historically went along with those traditions. We can give up belief in God while not losing touch with a treasured heritage. (344)

In other words, we can cut down the tree and still treasure how the leaves shade the house in the late summer. Dawkins wants to hate the root, which is our Lord Himself, and somehow retain the fruit.

All this is to say that Dawkins is not a sheer atheist, not by a long shot. He still feels the gravitational pull of the Christian faith, particularly of Anglicanism. And because a man is more than the sum of the propositions he affirms in his head, this is highly significant.

I must assume some things here, but I think they are safe to assume. It is clear that Dawkins is a baptized Christian, brought up in the Anglican communion. I don't know if he was disciplined or excommunicated, but, given the state of the Anglican church, that is unlikely in the extreme. He is one who lost his faith and his way, but this does not change the covenantal obligation he still has (and obviously still *feels*) to the Church he grew up in. That obligation is objective—it has nothing to do with what Dawkins says he believes. He is a baptized Christian, which means he does not have the right to his unbelief. It means that Richard Dawkins has a covenantal obligation to repent by next Saturday night and return to communion on Sunday.

For American evangelicals, I have to translate. I am not saying here that Dawkins is saved, or that his hatred of God is somehow okay because he was baptized as an infant. I am saying that being a Christian has two levels. One is objective, like a man getting married.

The other is subjective, like a man loving his wife. In the Church, the former is sealed by the sacrament of baptism. The latter is sealed by the Holy Spirit when He converts our hearts so that we come to love God through Jesus. Richard Dawkins still has the former, and it still eats at him. He has never had the latter.

Use the illustration of marriage. Dawkins is like a man who got married and who had a covenantal obligation to remain with his wife, loving her. But for some reason, he lost that love and walked away from his obligation, discarding his covenantal vows. The subjective loss of love accounts for the walking away, but it does not justify it. Neither does the loss of love erase the obligation. At times he speaks of his previous attachment with affection, but at other times he remembers he has to justify his infidelity, and so the anger returns.

And this accounts for Dawkins's strange obsession with people saying things like "a Christian child." He spends a good portion of chapter nine on it (311), but it was a point he made early on in the book as well (3). This is worth mentioning because this is what was done to Richard Dawkins. He was baptized in infancy and brought up in the faith. He mentions that his parents taught him to think for himself, but at the same time they did commit him in certain ways, and Dawkins is still bothered by it. This is not irrational; he *ought* to be bothered by it. He *is* still obligated. It is strange that he has this degree of sensitivity, because almost no one talks this way about baptism anymore, or teaches this. But he feels it, nonetheless.

The water of his baptism has not yet evaporated. We should pray that he is increasingly bothered, and that he comes to the point of full and deep repentance.